Morning Chai with God
Inspirational Messages that Strengthen Your Faith

C. Chérie Hardy

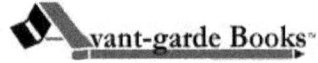

Avant-garde Books
Spiritual Division
Post Office Box 566
Mableton, Georgia 30126
www.avantgardebooks.net

Morning Chai with God
Inspirational Messages that Strengthen Your Faith

Copyright © 2015 and 2017 by Corendis Chérie Hardy
All rights reserved.

Portions of this manuscript are taken from the following published works by the author:

Daily Pearls: 365 Inspirational Quotes and Scriptures. Copyright © 2012.

Encouragement for the Grieving Heart: 365 Uplifting Quotes and Scriptures for Coping with Loss. Copyright © 2013.

The Power of Gratitude: 365 Quotes and Scriptures for Healing Your Mind, Body, and Heart. Copyright © 2013.

Love Doesn't Hurt: Life Lessons for Women. Copyright © 2003, 2009 and 2012.

Wise and Wonderful: Life Lessons for Single Mothers. Copyright © 2003, 2009 and 2012.

Some messages were previously published on the following website: ccheriehardy.com. Copyright © 2013-2014.

Scripture quotations marked (**AMP**) are taken the *Amplified® Bible*. Copyright © 1954, 1958, 1962, 1964, 1965, 1987 by The Lockman Foundation. Used by permission (**www.lockman.org**).

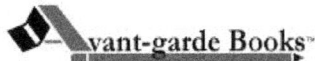

Avant-garde Books
Spiritual Division
Post Office Box 566
Mableton, Georgia 30126
www.avantgardebooks.net

Morning Chai with God
Inspirational Messages that Strengthen Your Faith

Copyright © 2015 and 2017 by Corendis Chérie Hardy
All rights reserved.

Scripture quotations marked (**ESV**) are taken from the *English Standard Version* of the Holy Bible. Copyright © 2001, 2007, and 2011 by Good News Publishers. Used by permission. All rights reserved.

Scripture quotations marked (**KJV**) are taken from the *King James Version* of The Holy Bible.

Scripture quotations marked (**NIV**) are taken from *The Holy Bible, New International Version*. Copyright © 1973, 1978, and 1984 by Biblica, Inc. Used by permission of Zondervan. All rights reserved worldwide.

Scripture quotations marked (**NKJV**) are taken from the *New King James Version*®. Copyright 1982 by Thomas Nelson, Inc. Used by permission. All rights reserved.

Scripture quotations marked (**NLT**) are taken from *The Holy Bible, New Living Translation*. Copyright © 1996, 2004, 2007. Used by permission of Tyndale House Publishers, Inc., Carol Stream, Illinois 60188. All rights reserved.

ISBN: 978-0-9908992-8-0

Cover Graphics: Suzanne Horwitz

This book is dedicated to my childhood friend,
Mary Filer

Thank you for helping the children!

"Don't worry about anything; instead, pray about everything. Tell God what you need, and thank him for all he has done. Then you will experience God's peace, which exceeds anything we can anything we can understand. His peace will guard your hearts and minds as you live in Christ Jesus."
—Philippians 4:6-7 (NLT)

Morning Chai with God
Inspirational Messages that Strengthen Your Faith

*Table of Contents

Author's Note	XI
Anger	1
Are You Asking God for the Right Things?	3
A Soft Answer	5
Be a Lighthouse	7
Can You Walk an Extra Mile?	8
Change the Channel	9
Confidence with God	12
Confront your Fears, not Abusers	14
Dealing with Fear	17
Disappointment	18
Don't Judge	20
Encouragement for the Grieving Heart	22
Encourage Children to Be Their Personal Best	24
Faith	25
Gaining Through Loss	26
Get D.E.E.P	28
Getting Out of Bad Relationships	30
Give, Just Do It!	32
God Has the Last Word	33
God Hears Your Prayers	36
God Never Stops Loving Us	37
God's Masterpiece	41
God's Provision	42
God's Voice	43

Morning Chai with God
Inspirational Messages that Strengthen Your Faith

*Table of Contents

Gratitude Changes Your Attitude	44
Guidance	45
Guilt	46
Healing	47
Help Is Available 24/7	48
His Pearl	49
Hope	50
Joy Comes in the Morning	51
Kick Bad Habits	52
Love Comes from God	53
Love in Action	54
Love Your Children Unconditionally	66
Mercy versus Meritocracy	68
Mothers Should Lead by Example	69
Pain, the Great Teacher	72
Perfect Peace	73
Pray Until Something Happens	74
Quit Blaming Others	75
Reconcile	77
Reflections on Motherhood	79
Rest in His Arms	81
Speak with Love Not Criticism	82
Stay in the Race	84
Strength	86
Supernatural Transformative Power	87
Talk to God about Your Children	89
That's What I'm Made For	91

Morning Chai with God
Inspirational Messages that Strengthen Your Faith

*Table of Contents

The Balanced Life	92
The First Step	95
The Last 12 Words of Jesus Christ	96
The Other Side of Through	98
The Power of Forgiveness	101
The Power of Memory	104
The Truth about Love	108
The Vine	114
Transformation	116
True Beauty	117
Value Your Time	119
Wait!	120
Welcome Positive Change	122
Whose Test Is It Anyway	123
Working as God's Agent	125
X-ray Your Heart	127
Yield to God	128
You Will Live	130
Zoom in on Self-Love	132
Acknowledgements	134
About the Author	135

*Taken from previously published works by the author.

Author's Note

"Faith is permitting ourselves to be seized by the things we do not see." — Martin Luther

Dear Reader:

Many years ago, I learned that faith is not always instantaneous. Great faith requires "heart" work and a selfless and unwavering commitment to serving God's kingdom. While talking about faith is easy, *walking* (living) in faith can potentially be one of the most challenging experiences we'll ever face.

Demonstrating faith means we take actions to accomplish something bigger than what we are able to achieve in own strength. In other words, the goal of our work is beyond our personal, physical, social, intellectual, and financial resources to complete. Through faith we carry knowledge in our heart that with God all things are possible. It isn't necessary to fully understand all the details because we trust that God will take care of everything along the way, and that the ultimate outcome of our actions is always in our favor for His glory.

Faith is always built and maintained by drawing closer to God. Our relationship with Him is strengthened through regular prayer, meditation, Bible study, personal consecration, fellowship with other believers, as well as listening to, and reading inspirational messages. In other words, it is unlikely that faith will come through happenstance and/or serendipity, but rather through sincere dedication to God and intentional effort. This is the faith that allows us to embrace His unfailing love, grace, joy, peace and so much more.

Author's Note

In *Morning Chai with God*, I share transformative and uplifting messages relating to some of life's most important issues, including love, forgiveness, anger, perseverance, etc. Each lesson comes directly from the wisdom I've gained during my own personal journey of faith. Many of these messages have been previously published in my books and on my website. It is my heartfelt prayer that these divinely-inspired lessons encourage you, and bring to closer to the true, *Author and Finisher* of your faith.

Beloved, be encouraged that God is with you no matter what season in life you are experiencing; He is faithful to give you a joyful heart; sound mind, and a preternatural peace even during life's most difficult storms.

Remember, our Heavenly Father doesn't change life, He changes us. Every experience has the potential to make us better, wiser, stronger, and more compassionate and loving when we choose to let our faith in a loving Creator be greater than our fear of loss and suffering. Unpleasant seasons in our life are inevitable, but through faith in Him, we can enjoy victorious living and triumph over trouble and tribulation.

With love,

C. Chérie Hardy

Morning Chai with God
Inspirational Messages that Strengthen Your Faith

C. Chérie Hardy

Anger

"Be angry, and do not sin: do not let the sun go down on your wrath, nor give place to the devil." — Ephesians 4:26-27 (NKJV)

Emotions are fleeting because they come and they go. Negative ones, like anger, become weakened as we focus on positive emotions like love and forgiveness. The more we meditate on the good, the less likely the bad will destructively dominate our lives.

Anger is an emotion that all human beings will experience. However, it is imperative that we don't let it become a raging spirit that can cause us to hurt ourselves and others. The first action for dealing with anger is asking God to remove it from our hearts.

Our Heavenly Father is willing and able to open our spiritual eyes to help us see whatever is necessary to let go of anger. We will learn that anger only destroys the person who is harboring it. Taking action with anger in our hearts will only make things worse, and cause us to lose more than we already have. Moreover, succumbing to anger means we relinquish our power and dignity. If anger controls us, our enemies can defeat us.

Another way of dealing with anger is using it to build rather than to tear down. In other words, anger can be a catalyst for improving how we do things. Beloved, use anger to constructively change bad situations. Rather than doing something to hurt yourself and or others, work to transform what you think is wrong. Let your anger motivate you to positively change whatever caused it.

Remember, anger is only dangerous when we hold it in our hearts instead of releasing it completely to God. What we do with our anger will determine if we make things better or

Anger

worse. Therefore, petition God to help you use your anger to heal painful situations and solve problems.

God already knows what happened to you. He is omniscient and sees everything that manifests in your life. He is a just God and will move on your behalf when the time is right. Keep your eyes on Him and his grace, and your anger will slowly start to dissipate.

Lastly, God has given you free will to choose your response. It pleases Him to see you taking an unpleasant circumstance and using it to help others. Everything will work out in your favor when you continue to honor Him and do the right thing. "For the wrath of man does not produce the righteousness of God." —James 1:20 (NKJV)

"The discretion of a man makes him slow to anger, and his glory to overlook a transgression." — Proverbs 19:11 (NKJV)

Are You Asking God for the Right Things?

"You ask and do not receive because you ask wrongly, to spend it on your passions." —James 4:3 (ESV)

Are your prayer requests mostly about material things or spiritual gifts? When you ask God for money are your asking for the wisdom about how to righteously use it and/or keep it? Is the money mainly about fulfilling a divine purpose or is it solely for your carnal pleasure?

When you ask God for promotion are you asking for Him to keep you humble and focused on serving others? When you ask for success are you asking God how you can use it to expand and uplift His kingdom? When you ask for healing are you asking God to teach you lessons through sickness?

When you ask God for companionship are you asking Him to make you a blessing for that person? Is what you're asking for ultimately going to lead you closer to God or take you further away? Are you fully prepared to handle what you're praying for?

Whatever we ask God for it should bring us closer to Him. It should help us improve the lives of people in God's kingdom. Our blessings are always for God's glory and honor. Instead of asking God for what makes us feel good, we should be inspired to ask for the things that will help us *do* good. The bottom line is we should pray for what God wants us to have; we should ask for His will to be completed in our lives.

Are You Asking God for the Right Things?

God wants us to have the best that life can offer, but He also wants us to remain humble and focused on pleasing Him. He doesn't want the acquisition of things to dominate our goals. We are placed on Earth to serve God's people. Having an abundance of things is a by-product of demonstrating excellence in whatever we do as well as His anointing and grace on our lives. However, we must never let things be the focus on life.

Everything we have is for His purpose and glory. And, we should always pray with that idea in our hearts. The good news is that God is faithful and will supply all of our needs and so much more , "but seek first the kingdom of God and His righteousness, and all these things shall be added unto you." — Matthew 6:33 (NKJV)

A Soft Answer

"A soft answer turneth wrath: but grievous words stir up anger." — Proverbs 15:1 (KJV)

Antoinette Tuff's personal story made the headlines of the national news after a man with a loaded gun walked into her place of employment, a school filled with children. With the grace of God, she managed to alter the outcome of a potentially fatal situation. No one doubts that she possibly saved countless lives by her compassionate and encouraging response to a sick man's madness. Ms. Tuff's actions reveals how the following ancient scripture is self-evident: "A soft answer turneth away wrath: but grievous words stir up anger." — Proverbs 15:1 (KJV)

It is inevitable that all of us will interact with difficult, disrespectful, and hostile people. While anger and retaliation might be the quickest response, it's not the right one. Ms. Tuff's example reminds us how using compassion, kindness, and patience is more effective for disarming an enemy rather than harshness and apathy.

We should ask God to teach us how to communicate with love, empathy, and sympathy, even to the most disagreeable person. While we should not condone bad behavior, we must keep in mind that there is a cause to every effect. We've heard the following cliché countless times, "Hurt people, hurt people." This is usually true and there is often a very sad story behind the scenes of hurtful people's lives.

I am one of those people who believes that monsters are not born, but made through terrible circumstances. At the same time, I believe that the quality of our lives is determined by the choices we make. Unfortunately, most people don't know that, and until they discover the grace and healing

A Soft Answer

power of God, they will act out in ugly ways. Our response to their behavior has the ability to change the narrative of their lives.

As believers, we must give broken people the same allowances we need or ourselves. Because we need forgiveness, we must give it to others. It's generally difficult to understand other people's behavior when we haven't journeyed in their shoes. However, whenever we take a moment to consider the suffering people have endured, we have the potential to become more sensitive and considerate and less judgmental. We shouldn't excuse bad behavior, but we should be slow to condemn people without understanding.

"Brothers, if anyone is caught in any transgression, you who are spiritual should restore him in a spirit of gentleness. Keep watch on yourself, lest you too be tempted." —Galatians 5:1 (ESV)

Be a Lighthouse

"Jesus said, "In the same way, let your light shine before others, that they may see your good deeds and glorify your Father in heaven." — Matthew 5:16 (NIV)

God has given each of us gifts to be used to empower everyone in His kingdom, including ourselves. These gifts are the things He equipped us with when He created the Earth and all that is in it. In other words, we were born with special gifts. With God's help, we can release our divine gifts and make things around us better. Our gifts move from within and are manifested outwardly.

Additionally, our gifts are like light; they illuminate and brighten any environment we enter. It doesn't make sense to hide them. Remember, light is needed to shine and overshadow darkness. Therefore, we must let our light shine (the spiritual gifts inside us), and be a lamp so all can see God's glory through our lives.

We must regularly ask God to show us when, where and how to fulfill His divine purpose. Note that empowering others will usually involve sacrifice. In other words, we will likely be inconvenienced and/or taken out of our comfort zones when God expects us to use our gifts.

However, God is faithful to give us strength, courage, and love to act on His behalf. It is our trust in Him that will allow us to complete His assigned tasks. It pleases Him when we make the intentional effort to use what He has divinely put into us. We must shine, and God will shine brighter.

"And let us not grow weary while doing good, for in due season we shall reap if we do not lose heart." — Galatians 6:9 (NKJV)

Can You Walk an Extra Mile?

"And whoever compels you to go one mile, go with him two." — Matthew 5:41 (NKJV)

No man can experience genuine and long-lasting success without the help and guidance of others. God works through people, not rocks and trees. Therefore, we must remember the words of Jesus Christ when He implores us to go the extra mile for others. Just keep in mind that this is rarely easy or convenient, but it is possible when we call upon the Lord for help.

Whenever we are called to be a sojourner in someone's life, we must be willing to sacrifice our time and resources. Even if the people we help can't or won't repay us for our effort, we are called by God to do what is right. When we please our Heavenly Father, when we allow ourselves to become vessels of His goodness, love, and grace.

There were many times in my life when I succumbed to my fatigue and didn't lend my support as I could (and should) have. Today, I make a greater effort to be there for others (if they've asked for my help) even when it interrupts my own personal agenda. I've learned that God is willing and able to strengthen us to go the extra mile whenever it is a part of our divine purpose.

The key is to starve our weaknesses and indolence and feed our faith to do what God has commissioned us to do. This requires continual communication with God through prayer, in addition to fasting and fellowship with others. In the end, God will give us the stamina and longsuffering to serve His kingdom. We are promised that "He gives strength to the weary and increases the power of the weak." — Isaiah 40:29 (NIV)

Change the Channel

"You will keep him in perfect peace, whose mind is stayed on You, because He trusts in You." — Isaiah 26:3 (NKJV)

Memories are one of the most powerful aspects of our humanity. They are stored in the brain's hard drive for the rest of our lives, and can only be deleted through disease and/or death. Even though we can determine on which thoughts we will focus, memories from the past will always resurface, and sometimes when we least expect it.

Thankfully, we have the divine gift to decide which channel or thoughts will be played in our mind. In other words, we can choose what we think about. If we don't like the channel that is playing, we can change it. We have the authority to re-direct our thoughts to something else, particularly something pleasant. We can replace a bad memory with a good one from the past or choose to dream about something positive we envision for the future.

Let's say a woman is driving to work and suddenly she has a bad memory of her mother's boyfriend sexually molesting her. Rather than suffer and mentally relive the ugly moment, she can literally tell her brain to shift to a joyful experience, such as going on vacation, accomplishing a goal, volunteering for her favorite charity or something as simple as sipping on a good cup of coffee.

If the woman presses the "fast forward" button in her brain, she can visualize herself doing something wonderful in the future. She can invoke images from her heart's desires and allow the sensation of joy to permeate throughout her brain and body. For example, the woman might hope to go to Egypt to see the ancient pyramids. She already has a picture of what they look like so she intentionally projects that image in her mind to interrupt and replace an unpleasant thought. She can

Change the Channel

make this more enjoyable as she pictures herself sharing the experience with someone she loves.

There is really no limit to what we can imagine. We don't have to become paralyzed by bad experiences; we don't have to become prisoners of our past if we decide to focus on the beautiful future God has planned for us.

Many years ago, I was divinely led to create a "bank of good thoughts" in order to protect my mind from bad memories. Today, whenever my spiritual enemy tries to mentally and emotionally attack me, I withdraw from the bank. I imagine myself doing something positive, especially something that I am passionate about. I even let myself imagine God hugging me. I call His essence to come close to me. There are times when it seems that I can actually feel His positive energy emanating around me.

God designed our minds like a remote control. It is a blessing that we can choose the subject matter of our ruminations and focus. A dark thought might "pop up", but we can block it.

Learning how to control our thoughts takes spiritual work, time, and patience, but it is worth the effort. God is willing to teach us how to change the channel. We can also ask God to heal our memories. He is faithful to show us that because of His grace, our problems and trouble didn't destroy us.

Our testimony is built on remembering that the enemy's hand was not successful because we are still here. God kept us safe, alive, and well. The lessons from the pain of our past have made us stronger, wiser, and more confident in God's love for us. Therefore, we can release bitterness and

Change the Channel

can face memories without fear because they are a reminder that we are more than conquerors!

Today, beloved, I encourage you to start strengthening your mind by depositing into your good-thought memory bank. Our lives are the result of our thoughts. The more we mentally set goals and take actions towards the future, the less likely we will focus on the past that is gone forever, and can never change.

God created imagination as a gift for us. We can use it to design our dreams and godly desires. The more we visualize enjoying the good life God has created for us, the more likely the desires of our heart will manifest into reality. Instead of letting bad memories haunt and torture us, we must learn to use all dimensions of the brain God has given to us. There is a part that can override ugly memories and allow us to meditate of God's love. Whenever we do this, painful memories from the past become smaller and less powerful to inhibit us from living abundantly through God's amazing grace.

"For I know the plans I have for you, declares the Lord. [I have] plans to prosper you and not to harm you, plans to give you hope and a future." —Jeremiah 29:11 (NIV)

Confidence with God

"For You [O Lord], formed my inward parts; You covered me in my mother's womb. I will praise You, for I am fearfully and wonderfully made. Marvelous are Your works, and that my soul knows well." — Psalm 139:13-14 (NKJV)

Being a high school teacher for almost 30 years gave me a better understanding of how we evolve as confident human beings. During adolescence, many people are so busy trying to "fit in" and be accepted by others, they inadvertently oppress their divine uniqueness and fail to develop and grow confident in their own skin.

When people don't learn to be comfortable with themselves in spite of their weaknesses and imperfections, they often lack the confidence to feel good about their personal identity — the way God made them.

In order to change this, we must align our self-image according to how God sees us. The *world* doesn't encourage us to have a multidimensional view of beauty, talent, and intelligence, but God does. That's why He created each person with a one-of-a-kind set of finger prints as well as body scent. Difference is His specialty — His signature on our humanity, but people often miss the power of this because they embrace the distortions of the world, which promotes being like everyone else.

Beloved, I encourage you to resist uniformity and get true confidence by seeing yourself through God's eyes. He fearfully and wonderfully made you, and wholeheartedly embracing this truth is the only way to become a strong and whole person. A relationship with Him helps us to make peace about who we are; it allows us to be true to ourselves

Confidence with God

without the unhealthy need to be approved by people, especially those who don't positively contribute to our lives.

The stronger our relationship with God, the less likely we will get distracted, frustrated, or angry when people don't respect and accept us as unique individuals. When we waste valuable time focusing on how people judge us, we take our eyes off our own goals. This can potentially delay or inhibit us from accomplishing our God-given purpose.

To be confident, we must look to the God who created us from His love and pleasure. He gave us our physical features and personality. Our destiny is truly in His hands, not our critics. While constructive criticism can be empowering and make us wiser and better in various dimensions of our lives, negative, unmerited persecution should not be internalized. You can use it as a stepping stone, but don't let it become a stumbling block to your human growth and development.

At some point, in our lives, people will not like us. They might judge us and/or condemn us, but what God thinks matters the most. While people ae putting you down, answer them with your actions, not words. Keep being productive, helping others and doing your best, and let God do the rest.

Finally, make sure your heart is in the right place with your Heavenly Father. When God is pleased with you and you know it, you can achieve extraordinary things for His kingdom.

"For the LORD does not see as man sees; for man looks at the outward appearance, but the LORD looks at the heart." —I Samuel 16:7b (NKJV)

Confront Your Fears, Not Abusers

"Some people believe holding on and hanging in there are signs of great strength. However, there are times when it takes much more strength to know when to let go and then do it."
— Ann Landers

Some social scientists believe it is cathartic to confront the people who hurt you. However, this can potentially exacerbate a bad situation. When we confront abusive people—people who could not be paid to apologize for hurting others—we really work against ourselves and them. Some abusers will go to their graves denying and/or justifying, trivializing and minimizing their actions. Confronting them turns on their faulty defense mode and can bring out the worst of their behavior.

Only when abusers have healed themselves from their shame can they admit the truth. Be aware that they may never take ownership of the pain they caused. Just remember that what they did to you is between them and God. God only holds us responsible for *our* actions. We must use our faith to move out of the way so He can deal with abusers. We should regularly pray for them with the passion and hope that we have for ourselves, but we must let them go.

Beloved, do not allow the lack of an apology stop you from being happy. Confront your own fears. *Why are you afraid of leaving an abusive relationship? Are you afraid of being alone?* Do you really think that you will be less happy if you let someone go?

When you confront your fears you begin to excavate the truth buried under the layers of pain. The truth is you can choose not to be a victim; you have the power to change your circumstances. Acceptance of abuse is a sign that there are

Confront Your Fears, Not Abusers

issues you must work to change. You only delay your healing when you fail to confront the fears deep inside of you.

First, ask God for guidance about how to get out of an abusive relationship. Sometimes walking away is not simple, especially when you're biologically connected to the people who hurt you. Letting go doesn't mean you don't love them or you haven't forgiven those who hurt you. However, it does mean that you are committed to honoring and valuing yourself enough not to become someone else's human punching bag or dart board.

While some people can have VIP status in our lives, others must be kept in the balcony. Don't feel guilty about not allowing negative, toxic people in close proximity because they will maliciously hurt you every chance they get. This problem exists of how they feel about themselves; it has nothing to do with you. No matter what you've done, you are not put on this Earth to be in someone's torture chamber.

Resolve to let go of people who intentionally hurt you. At first this will seem impossible because bonds are not easily broken, however at some point, you will begin to enjoy a peace beyond human comprehension when you stand up for yourself and refuse to allow toxic people to poison your atmosphere.

Breaking a bond with a someone with whom we've had a close and/or long-term relationship isn't easy, even if the person maliciously hurt us. And, it's more difficult for an abuser to let go. People who find pleasure in hurting others don't like not having victim available. In some cases, leaving attempt to leave will trigger an abuser to take his or her evil to another level. Tragically, this can even lead to murder.

Therefore, it is imperative that you pray about the safest way of getting out of your situation. It is likely that you

Confront Your Fears, Not Abusers

will need a well-thought out plan in addition to a network of people to support you as you transition to a new life. (Read my book, *Breaking Bonds*.)

Decide before you leave that you will never go back. Pray that bitterness and resentment will not consume your heart. And, do not feel guilty about the failure of the broken relationship. Not allowing an abuser in your life doesn't mean you haven't forgiven him or her; it doesn't mean you're angry. On the contrary, it shows that you have a healthy sense of self-worth and you understand that God wants you to surround yourself with people who appreciate and respect you.

Jesus taught that we should love our enemies; do good to those who hate us; bless those who curse us; and pray for those who mistreat us (Luke 6:27-28). However, God doesn't get any glory from us suffering from injury or being killed. None of His commandments require that we allow ourselves to be abused.

While it's ideal to be at peace and on good terms with every person in our lives, sometimes we have to love, do good, bless and pray for people from a distance. Remaining in a close relationship with abusive people is too dangerous. Love them; hope the best for them, but let them go.

Dealing with Fear

"The fear of man brings a snare: but whoso puts his trust in the LORD shall be safe." — Proverbs 29:25

Loss can often evoke feelings of fear, especially after the death of a beloved person. The person's mortality can make us more aware and thoughtful about our own. Anxiety about the unknown makes us feel uncomfortable and frightful. However, worrying about we don't understand will not improve our circumstances.

We don't get better by meditating on possible bad things that can happen to us. The truth is that problems are inevitable, but God is with us through it all. He will comfort and guide us through the pain. The antidote for fear is faith. The more we strengthen our faith, the less fearful we become.

As I have already mentioned in this text, building our faith takes time and effort. The notion of being strong during painful circumstances is easy in the movies, but much more difficult in reality. Moreover, faith doesn't completely erase fear because it is a human emotion. The key for victorious living is to not allow fear to become a spirit, something that consumes your entire faith. The good news is that our faith in God will override our emotions and gives us the courage to live fully in spite of our trouble.

Nurturing our faith instead of fear helps us to believe that everything will be alright — things will work out for our good. Through faith, we know God is working on our behalf whether we can feel it or see it.

Jesus taught that we should "not let our heart be troubled, neither be afraid because he would give us peace." (John 14: 27) We must have faith that He will keep His promises. This will lead to releasing the spirit of fear.

Disappointment

"Not that I was ever in need, for I have learned to be content with whatever I have. I know how to live on almost nothing or with everything. I have learned the secret of living in every situation, whether it is with a full stomach or empty, with plenty or little. For, I can do everything through Christ who gives me strength." — Philippians 4:11-13 (NLT)

At the heart of all frustration is disappointment. This occurs when a particular outcome is not what we desired or expected. We will always be disappointed when we are more concerned about fulfilling "our" will, instead of God's. Surrendering to God's providence is one way we can release the obsession of wanting something we cannot (or should not) have. Accepting that He knows what is best for us can heal our hearts and minds.

There are also two other things you can do whenever you are plagued with disappointment: (1) set out to get what you want if you think you can, or (2) make peace about not having what you want. In other words, decide to be content and grateful even if you never get the object of your desire. Believe that whatever is in God's will must manifest in your life at the right time.

God will open doors that no man can shut; He will close doors that no man can open. He is your biggest cheerleader. There is no need to be disappointed when you can't have your way. Our loving Heavenly Father is faithful to protect, provide and guide you in the right direction. He will meet all of your needs. Trusting Him and not leaning on your own understanding will transform disappointment into gratitude.

Disappointment

Furthermore, if you have lived without something or someone before, you can keep living without it now. Sometimes not having what we think we want is a blessing dressed up like something else; sometimes what we have lost will never reappear in our lives, and that's the best thing that could ever happen to us. If we make peace that loss is a natural and inevitable part of life, we will reduce our chances of experiencing unnecessary disappointment.

We must also accept that God isn't less loving or powerful because this happens. God knows that disappointment is one of the greatest tools to teach us gratitude, patience, and wisdom. Sometimes He withholds some of our desires to protect us from harm.

Our loving Heavenly Father sees the pitfalls that we don't. Learn to thank God for not answering your prayers exactly the way you asked. If you could only see all that He is shielding you from, you would not be disappointed.

Don't Judge

"Do not judge and you will not be judged. Do not condemn and you will not be condemned. Forgive and you will be forgiven." — Luke 6:37 (NIV)

Through faith we can train ourselves to first try to understand others rather than judging them. This means we should refrain from forming conclusions without knowledge of facts and all aspects of issues. We cannot believe that we are intelligent if we don't consider factors that might not be evident on the surface, but are important parts of the whole issue. Our perspective will never be fair and accurate if we fail to look beyond what we see.

One of my high school English teachers once said, "Believe none of what you hear, and only half of what you see." It took some time, but as a mature adult, I fully understand the meaning of that cliché. There is always a story behind the scenes that don't capture the entire explanation for what is in front of us. However, God, and only Him, knows all the intricate details of a situation. He knows we can't. Judging a person would be unfair, unjust, and according to God, unrighteous.

Someone I love made a very terrible choice that impacted (and will continue) to have negative consequences. Of course, I would never condone wrong doing, but once I discovered all of the details of what happened, I was able to have more compassion and empathy for this person.

There are so many layers of our character and being. God takes the time to consider these things and has mercy on us. No, He doesn't condone sin. However, He chooses to look beyond our faults and love us anyway. When we judge people, it is difficult to love them unconditionally. We must

Don't Judge

emulate our Heavenly Father by demonstrating longsuffering and mercy for people.

Judgment causes people to condemn and put down rather than encourage, forgive, and instill the idea that transformation is possible when there is faith and hope in something greater than our humanity — God.

The cure for judgment is to always remember how we would want to be treated regardless of my mistakes and flaws. I don't know anyone who hasn't fallen short and didn't need a second chance. The same grace and love we want for ourselves should inspire us to give it to others.

"Your love for one another will prove to the world that you are my disciples." — John 13:35 (NLT)

Encouragement for the Grieving Heart

"Blessed are those who mourn, for they shall be comforted."
—Matthew 5:4 (NKJV)

Life is like the weather. There are bright sunny days when butterflies decorate the sky and we smile and laugh with blissful glee, yet there are also cold days when the winds rage and life's heavy, cold torrential rains feel like stones descending upon us. Loss is a season, too which all of us must bear.

During this dark time, we must wrap ourselves with God's love to endure the pain. It is God who covers us with His amazing love even though we lose people, and things just like the trees lose their leaves in autumn. However, after loss there is always gain.

While our beloved is irreplaceable, we are always blessed with a season of warmth, renewal and regeneration. And, just as the flowers do in spring, we bloom with beauty and grace—defying the harshness of the wintery days which we longed to pass.

It might be difficult, but we must accept that some aspects of loss can never be understood. They will forever remain an unsolved mystery to us—inexplicable no matter how hard we try to make sense of things.

Therefore, we must make peace that while we cannot explain or rationalize the pain from loss, we can overcome it by trusting God, the Creator of Heaven and Earth. Living victoriously, in spite of no longer possessing what we hold dear, is our vindication for loss's attempt to break and/or destroy us.

Encouragement for the Grieving Heart

Yes, through the grace of God we can move on and use loss for our personal growth; we can use our pain for a purpose. Our strength, resolve and sinew can become powerful and inspirational lessons, especially for others, to stand tall in the midst of life's emotional hurricanes, tornadoes and floods.

While rising above the unforgettable moments of loss is possible, it is not easy. Overcoming our grief is not spontaneous and automatic. Moreover, time doesn't necessarily heal all wounds, but it lessens the sting. There will always be scars from loss, but one day those wounds become old and more tolerable to bear. Serenity only comes because we make peace that loss is an aspect of life that we can never change. It is how things are supposed to be — loss is not a mistake or an anomaly.

We must embrace the idea that loss is an inevitable part of life, and God doesn't change life, He changes us. In other words, no matter who we are, regardless of race, religious affiliation, socioeconomic status, education, etc., all humans will share some of the same experiences — including loss. We can become stronger, wiser, more compassionate, and become humbler as a result of loss. These are rich treasures that are often buried deep beneath the discomfort that loss brings to our hearts and minds.

Encourage Children to Be Their Personal Best

"And [Jesus] took the children in His arms, placed His hands on them and blessed them." — Mark 10:16 (NIV)

When my daughter was growing up, I never encouraged her to compete with other children. I repeatedly coached her to do her personal best at all times. Competing with her own self was a better way to monitor and assess her progress. Over the years, I had seen so many examples of unhealthy competition. This resulted in me teaching my daughter that it is exhausting trying to outdo someone else.

When you strive to be "the best", your focus is on performing better than someone else. Therefore, when you're not number one you feel inferior and defeated. I am grateful that my daughter embraced this idea. I believe it alleviated undue stress and peer pressure from her life because her focus was on herself rather than other people.

Inculcate in your children's heart that they are just as intelligent, beautiful, worthy, etc. as any other child. Encourage them to do their personal best and not waste energy and time trying to conquer the world. If their personal best leads them to the top, fine. If it doesn't, it's still fine. You will take so much pressure off your children when you teach them to do their best and let God deal with the rest.

"Competition makes us faster; collaboration makes us better." — Unknown

Faith

"Now faith is the confidence of what we hope for and assurance of what we do not see." — Hebrews 11:1 (NIV)

Faith allows us to trust that God knows what He is doing and will help us understand what we are going through. Every experience gives us a chance to strengthen our faith. It involves a conviction and choice to tap into the spiritual capital and potential that rests within us.

Nurturing our faith through sincere and intimate communication with God reminds us of the divine blessings and limitless possibilities that we cannot see with our physical eyesight. This knowing faith creates an unwavering assurance that God is working on our behalf even though we are hurting and afraid.

Faith in God means willingly surrender to His perfect plan for every dimension of our lives. It reminds us that He will always comfort us and supply what we need.

"Trust in Lord with all your heart, and lean not on your own understanding; in all your ways acknowledge Him, and He shall direct your paths." –Proverbs 3:5-6 (NKJV)

Gaining Through Loss

"Blessed are those who mourn for they shall be comforted."
— Matthew 5:4 (NKJV)

    Many experiences that we endure in life, particularly losing the people and things we cherish most, are beyond our control. There are circumstances which are unavoidable and there is nothing we can do to prevent them in our own finite, limited power, no matter how hard we try.

    Therefore, it is paramount that we lean on what is greater than ourselves — God, Our Creator of Everything. He designed the blueprint for life which includes both gain and loss; good and bad; and darkness and light. God is not less great or loving because we face difficult moments. All of our pain is a part of the fabric of life, and adversity is integrally woven into our journey.

    We must be comforted that God never wastes our pain because He loves us. With His help, we learn that there are rich spiritual treasures beneath all of our tribulation. These special gems allow us to become more loving, compassionate, grateful, generous, thoughtful, etc.

    I cannot reiterate enough that God doesn't change life, He changes us. No one can avoid going through rough seasons. However, through faith, we are able frame how we *see* our circumstances. Deeper and intimate fellowship with God helps us to understand that loss always brings us closer to Him. There is always a reason for every experience we have and through Him we get understanding.

    After loss, we must petition God to comfort us. We should also ask Him to show us what we can learn from our pain. He is faithful to answer our prayers if we decide to embrace His sovereignty and trust Him. Spring comes after

Gaining Through Loss

any dark season of loss. There is always gain in some form. Let us express our gratitude in word and in deed to our Heavenly Father for His providence in our lives.

"And after you have suffered a little while, the God of all grace, who has called you to his eternal glory in Christ, will himself restore, confirm, strengthen, and establish you." — I Peter 5:10 (ESV)

Get DEEP (Drop Everything and Enter Prayer)

"Now it came to pass in those days that He [Jesus] went out to the mountain to pray and continued all night in prayer to God." — Luke 6:12 (NKJV)

The key to greater intimacy with God is communication (prayer). The good news is that we have access to God's ear 24/7. He is never too busy to listen to us. He doesn't treat us like objects by picking us up and putting us down whenever it is convenient. God cares and He wants us to talk to Him and He wants to speak to our hearts. Moreover, what we tell Him is kept confidential; and safe from condemnation and ridicule.

Jesus's life is an example of the results of fervent, regular prayer. We learn through Him that we can gain power, insight, strength, courage, faith and peace by talking to God. Personally, I have found that prayer doesn't instantly change my circumstances most times, but I do feel immeasurable peace and comfort knowing that God heard my concerns and that He is willing and able to do abundantly above what I ask for and think about.

Be encouraged that we don't have to try to connect all the dots; understand every problem; and carry every burden. Let us take what is in our hearts to a loving and compassionate God who has time for us no matter how many other things He is doing. That's why He's God! He distinguishes himself by doing what we cannot.

Beloved, never doubt that God is faithful to comfort you through any situation. With prayer, He will reveal to us everything we need to know to keep going when we want to give up and hold on when we are close to letting go. Prayer helps us to forgive; it helps us to move past fear so that it

Get DEEP (Drop Everything and Enter Prayer)

won't hijack us. It's true: prayer changes us and it transforms our circumstances.

So, turn off your phone and go boldly to God's throne in prayer. Tell God about every secret thing—withhold nothing from Him. God will put solutions to your issues in your heart. He will direct your paths. Listen to His voice and above all, trust Him, the One who cannot fail. Just watch and wait to see the manifestations of His love for you.

"I will lift my eyes to the hills—from whence comes my help? My help comes from the LORD, who made heaven and earth." —Psalm 121:1-2 (NKJV)

Getting Out of Bad Relationships

"For the righteous fall seven times and rises again..."
-Proverbs 24:26a (ESV)

I personally know all too well that while it is important to do whatever we can to avoid *getting in* bad relationships, an even greater lesson is having the courage to *get out* of them. Unfortunately, too many of us stay unhappily married and endure long-term maltreatment because it is financially convenient or because they don't want to be embarrassed by the failure of the relationship.

Many of us have paid a hefty price, emotional, spiritually, physically for deciding not to leave a toxic relationship. The continual fighting, disrespect and chaos eventually takes a toll on both our physical and mental health. I have witnessed firsthand, women suffer from chronic diseases and disorders due to the stress of having to cope with loveless and tumultuous lives. However, the greatest casualties of these unhealthy unions are the children who also suffer because of their parents' selfish choices.

Fortunately, this doesn't have to happen. Focusing on faith, instead of fear allows us to let go of bad relationships, especially after we have done all we can to resolve issues without success. "Getting out" is often the most difficult and complicated decision that we must make, but sometimes it is the most effective choice for having peace, sanity and filled with love and mutual respect for every member of the environment.

Getting Out of Bad Relationships

Remember, we will never change what we accept. Also, we teach people how to treat us. If we tolerate the worst of someone's behaviour, we will never experience his/her best. Sometimes, people will be inspired to do better because they value us and don't want to lose us. Of course, amazing things can happen when we are willing to learn "how to love" God's way and thus, improve the quality of our relationships.

"Restore to me the joy of your salvation, and uphold me with a willing spirit." — Psalm 51:12 (ESV)

Give. Just Do It!

"Give, and you will receive. Your gift will return to you in full--pressed down, shaken together to make room for more, running over, and poured into your lap. The amount you give will determine the amount you get back."
—Matthew 6:38 (NLT)

    I often teach young people that **in life we don't often get what we want; we get what we give.** Whatever you give will come back to you. When you give love, it comes back. When you give joy, it is returned. When you give mercy, you receive mercy. When you give patience, you will experience it from others for yourself. Give good gifts to others, regardless of what they do to you. Distinguish yourself as a child of God by choosing not to be vindictive.

    Lastly, give your burdens and fears to God. Resign as supervisor of the universe and give God back His job. He will give you peace, hope, joy, love… God may not give you everything you want, but He will supply all of your needs. Give Him the authority to decide what is best for you.

    "Each of you should give what you have decided in your heart to give, not reluctantly or under compulsion, for God loves a cheerful giver." –2 Corinthians 9:7 (NIV)

God Has the Last Word

"… Indeed, let God be true but every man a liar. As it is written: 'That You may be justified in Your words, and may overcome when You are judged.'" –Romans 3:4 (NKJV)

It's very easy to be distracted and discouraged by the negative proclamations people make about us. However, when we keep our attention on God and nurture our faith, we can have comfort knowing that God has the final word. We can have rest and peace knowing that God always ends on a good note. We are triumphant through Him who loves us.

Whatever the Lord says about our lives is all that matters. There are people who received a negative report from the doctor, but they believed God made the human body and therefore was the Ultimate Physician who could heal them. Some people grew up in homes where their self-worth was discounted and they were repeatedly told that they wouldn't succeed for one reason or another, yet these people went on to do extraordinary things with God's guidance and help.

I personally believe that God gets great pleasure in using the remnant, the underdog, the unloved… to manifest His incomparable glory. "…Let the weak say, I am strong." –Joel 3:10 (ASV)

The following are three principal ways to stay focused on God. Of course, I could add many more powerful and useful strategies, but this will get you started until you can expand your own personal arsenal against your spiritual enemy.

Listen to spiritually, uplifting messages. I often teach young people that our lives are like vessels. Whatever we put into ourselves is what exists within us. Furthermore, it's the only thing that can come out of us. If you put in junk, that's

God Has the Last Word

what manifests outwardly as your actions. If you inculcate something that builds you up, you become stronger.

Never fail to listen to messages that edify your mind and spirit. Seek out churches in your local community that teach you how to establish and maintain a relationship with God. Additionally, there is a plethora of CD's available which target your specific area of need.

Interact with positive, loving people. Most of us have experienced being around people who help us to feel stronger, wiser, and more hopeful. At the same time, we know what the opposite feels like. It is imperative that we forge good relationships with people who focus on the positive aspects of life—those who strive to work to resolve issues rather than meditate on their problems.

Mentally and verbally affirm a desired outcome instead of ruminating about what's wrong. This strategy is highly effective for people who have been inundated with harmful, degrading messages about themselves. The long-term effects of negative conditioning usually lead to feelings of low self-worth and hopelessness. Healing comes when we replace each toxic message with the opposite.

For example, if you were told you were a moron, tell yourself you are intelligent and capable of doing great things. If someone said you weren't going to be successful, repeatedly say that you will rise above adversity and live victoriously because you are a child of The Most High God who fearfully and wonderfully made you to succeed. This really works!

As you flood out the negative thoughts, and fill yourself with positive ones, you become empowered to do what God has anointed and appointed you to do. You were made in your Heavenly Father's image; you are ONLY what He says you are.

God Has the Last Word

"So God created mankind in his own image, in the image of God he created them; male and female he created them." —Genesis 1:27 (NIV)

God Hears Our Prayers

After having a conversation which scratched the surface of some old wounds, I found myself fighting release the bitterness I felt. For quite some time, my mind was plagued with an issue that I had struggled to conquer. As I labored in prayer and gratitude throughout the night and early morning the next day, I decided that I would use my experience as a springboard for my weekly inspirational message.

Amazingly, when I started my morning devotion by watching a recording of my pastor, I discovered that his teaching was on the very subject I wanted to write about. Additionally, it was as if God was speaking directly to me and confirming all of the promises He'd made to me; and all the things that I believed in my heart about how my situation would turn out in the end.

I rejoiced in knowing that God had heard my cries. He was attentively and faithfully listening to me in the wee hours of the morning as I communicated my feelings to Him. Meditate on the following scriptures and believe that God hears you 24/7, 365 days per year!

"But verily God hath heard me; he hath attended to the voice of my prayer. Blessed by God, which hath not turned away my prayer, nor his mercy from me." — Psalm 66:19-20 (KJV)

"In the day of my trouble I will call upon thee: for thou wilt answer me." –Psalm 86:7 (KJV)

"He shall call upon me, and I will answer him: I will be with him in trouble; I will deliver him, and honour him." –Psalm 91:15 (KJV)

God Never Stops Loving Us

> "…and lo, I am with you always, even to the end of the age. Amen." — Matthew 28:20b (NKJV)

No matter how we judge the quality of our relationship with a parent, his/her death is usually quite difficult to handle. The biological and spiritual bonds that connect us run deep even if we were not close. A part of our parents remains with us throughout our entire lives. This is how God designed and ordained human life to be.

The death of my earthly father was a pivotal moment in my life. It forced me to reflect on some painful aspects of my childhood. The man whose DNA helped create me was forever gone, but ugly memories of being compared to him still lingered in my conscious. Although I can recall only a few times that we had had any personal interaction, I cannot forget the hundreds of times I was told how horrible he was. He was hated, demonized and often vilified as a "crazy", selfish and worthless monster. He was unloved and despised for not doing what he should have as a father and husband.

As one can imagine, it was even more devastating to hear these horrible things followed with being told that I was just like him—that I would eventually become as insane as he was. As a child, this was emotionally and psychologically detrimental because I had not yet developed the cognitive ability to sort through what was true or false about me. For many years, I believed and internalized that I was all the hideous names I had been repeatedly called.

I didn't understand that my true worth, and identity were not shaped by the person spouting out the filth, but the One who birthed me from His spirit. For years, I would often worry that on any given day I would suddenly become "crazy" and dysfunctional and end up in a mental institution.

God Never Stops Loving Us

Even though my life was, and had always been on an entirely directly path from my father's, I did recognize remnants of his personality in me. This frightened and shamed me more than all the verbal and emotional abuse I had ever endured.

Being like my father meant losing everything I dreamed and hoped for, and that haunted me into my adult years until I discovered the truth. And, even for a short time after his tragic death, I felt the stigma of being connected to a man who seemed to have wasted his life away — an underachiever who hadn't done anything for anyone, not even his children.

However, the last memory of my father is one that I will cherish for the rest of my life. Although I will not share the intimate details now, looking back it was not by chance or coincidence that I unexpectedly saw him looking so healthy and sane a few months before his passing. God wanted to heal me and that last, brief moment with my dad was like a warm kiss on my cheek.

One evening a few weeks after his death, I became overcome with grief about all the missed opportunities for reconciliation. I regretted that I had never known my father; I felt sad that I had only gotten a very small and distorted glimpse of the complex person he really was.

Now, I would never get the chance to patch things up between us. He was gone forever and I didn't have peace about the state of his soul. I cried out to God and began to pray for Him to help me let go of all the guilt and shame that was emotionally and spiritually crushing me.

Suddenly, I felt God's presence around me. God began to show me that my father was not *born* a monster. And, in

God Never Stops Loving Us

spite of his shortcomings, he had deserved and needed love. In fact, he needed a greater portion of love because of all the pain he had endured including growing up with an invalid mother and then later witnessing firsthand the horrors of the Vietnam War.

Moreover, he had never really been taught how to be a righteous man and a good father. He was a product of all he knew and had experienced. If he had known how to do more — to do what was right, he likely would have. Although my father's troubles didn't excuse the abdication of his responsibilities, understanding the details of the causes and effects of his life made me less bitter.

Today, I realize that the hate that was projected on him only made him feel worse about himself. I now know he must have felt defeated since it was often verbalized. He couldn't have given me and anyone else love because he didn't even have it for himself. This left him hopeless.

God also encouraged me to juxtapose a list of everything my father and I had completed throughout our lives. Doing this gave me a visual of how our lives had taken almost completely opposite paths. What I realized that our lives had had very difference outcomes because we hadn't been exposed to the same information and experiences. Even though I had shared some aspects of my father's personality, we were two unique and separate human beings.

The biggest blessing was the revelation that God had chosen the father He wanted me to have. There was something in my father that God needed me to inherit so that I could fulfill His divine purpose for my life. Thus, rejecting my father would mean not accepting my total self. There would

God Never Stops Loving Us

be no way I could ever feel complete unless I embraced all of me, including the parts that disquieted me.

I am so grateful that God comforted me by showing me real love is unconditional. Despite our flaws and mistakes, He sees us worthy of love. We should model His character and love people no matter what. We should forgive anyway; we should toil and labor to reconcile with those who desire it—those who commit to making amends.

I will never know the joy of having a healthy father-daughter relationship but I can pass along the lessons I learned from my mistakes. After all those years of trying to distance myself from my father's image, I now thank God on a continual basis for choosing my parents.

Even if circumstances limit the quality of the relationship you can have with people, cling to the hope that with God's amazing grace, all can be restored. God specializes in restoration, including relationships. He can resurrect what seems dead or lost forever. The key involves people cooperating with the Holy Spirit. People must put down their pride and let God do the work that they cannot.

Ask God to show you how to replace the ugliness of resentment and bitterness caused by selfishness with the beauty of prayer and blessings, but most importantly, with His love.

God's Masterpiece

"I will praise thee; for I am fearfully and wonderfully made: marvelous are thy works; and that my soul knoweth right well." –Psalm 139:14 (KJV)

    I believe that God equips each of us with the confidence and ability to do great things before we are even conceived by our parents. Before we are manifested on Earth, we are made in heaven by Him. Before the world began, we rested in God's womb. God cradled us in His bosom until we were released to our parents.

    I used to think that our self-worth is built from the outside. However, after observing children as an educator and mother, I now believe that we are born confident and comfortable in our own skin. Few of us keep that original sense of self-worth because it is stripped away due to negative experiences.

    Many of us are told (both directly and indirectly) that we are less than someone else's idea of beautiful, intelligent, special, etc. While God created us uniquely, the world promotes being followers of other people. As children of God, we must embrace the idea that He fearfully and wonderfully made us. He created our physical attributes and personality. Therefore, God made us just the way we are supposed to be. No matter what, we are beautiful, equipped, worthy and capable of fulfilling His divine purpose for us. When we see ourselves through God's eyes, we feel powerful and confident.

God's Provision

"Ask, and it will given to you; seek, and you will find; knock, and it will be opened to you. For everyone who asks receives, and he who seeks finds, and to him who knocks, it will be opened." — Matthew 7:7-8 (NKJV)

God is our loving Heavenly Father and we are His children. He delights in making sure we have whatever we need. It pleases Him to bless us. His glory shines brightly as people witness His work in our lives.

Never doubt that God will provide. Trust that He will give us more than we could ever ask for or imagine. All He wants is that we're committed to Him. He doesn't want to compete for attention. He doesn't want the cares of this world consume us and take us away from fellowship with Him.

Our faith in Him warms His heart. He has so much goodness stored up for us. He holds an infinite supply of goodness that overflows into our lives every day.

We can rejoice that Our Heavenly Father is rich with what we need to be strong and triumph over every trial and tribulation. We just have to ask Him and prepare to receive His gifts as well as believe that He is "able to do exceedingly above all that we ask or think, according to His power that works in us." (Ephesians 3:20)

God's Voice

"How sweet are Your words to my taste, *Sweeter* than honey to my mouth! Through Your precepts I get understanding; Therefore I hate every false way."
—Psalm 119:103-104 (NKJV)

Prayer, talking to God, is one facet of building and strengthening our faith. However, listening to God's voice in our hearts is equally important. When God is directing our actions, thoughts, and communication, we will move in the right direction. His words become the wisdom, love, and grace to do what is far too arduous in our own strength.

His voice also gives us peace in the midst of life's many storms. All we have to do is get in a secret place where there is no noise to distract us. This is when we can hear words sweeter than any dessert we've ever had.

We must let God's words supersede all others, including our own. This is the way to understand the knowledge and lessons necessary to fulfill God's will for us.

"It's in stillness, not busyness, that we tune our spiritual ears to hear the voice of God. The Lord always speaks to us in that still, small voice, but often it's drowned out amid all the turmoil of our daily lives." — Andrew Wommack

Gratitude Changes Your Attitude

"Give thanks in all circumstances; for this is the will of God in Christ Jesus for you."– I Thessalonians 5:18 (ESV)

    I love the following expression: "Every day might not be good, but there is good in every day." It's impossible to avoid difficult and unpleasant circumstances. Life is made of high and low seasons; peaceful and tumultuous moments; sad and joyful days. However, in spite of what we experience, there is always good in our lives. Sometimes that good is conspicuous and blatantly stares us in the face.
    On the other hand, goodness can be a treasure buried deep beneath our trials and tribulations. Nevertheless, there is always something to celebrate — something for which we should be thankful. When gratitude emanates from our heart, the less depressed, fearful and hopeless we will feel. We must train ourselves to focus more on what we already have rather than what we think in missing.
    As we let God know how much we appreciate what we have, what we have (the things He has blessed us with) will appreciate. Let us praise our Heavenly Father in all situations. Gratitude, especially in the midst of difficulty, confuses our spiritual enemy, but most importantly it pleases our God.
    "If your only prayer would be 'thank you' that would be enough" –Meister Eckhart

Guidance

"Show me your ways, O LORD; teach me your paths. Lead me in Your truth and teach me, for you are the God of my salvation; on You I will wait all the day."
–Psalm 25:4-5 (NKJV)

Most of the suffering I endured as an adult was a result of failing to follow God's guidance. I was misled by my own selfish desires and focused on *my* will instead of God's. I have learned the hard way that God is the ultimate spiritual navigation system.

Letting Him direct our paths; surrendering to His desires for us; and using His solutions are ways to avoid or minimize trouble and life's roadblocks. When we pray, and ask God for guidance, He is faithful to speak to our hearts and give us the right answers we seek. All we have to do (through faith) is trust Him.

He will not lead us to life's dead-ends and traffic jams. Because of His perfect love, He will lead us safely to the destinations of our divine purpose. Moreover, His guidance will teach us great lessons on how to use our experiences with loss to gain wisdom, love, freedom, and power. So activate the real GPS (God's Positioning System)!

"The name of the LORD is a strong tower; the righteous run to it and are safe." — Proverbs 18:10 (NKJV)

Guilt

"Create in me a clean heart, O God; and renew a right spirit within me." –Psalm 51:10 (KJV)

Guilt can occur for a myriad of reasons. It's possible for people to feel guilty about not having done or said things, particularly before a loss. Also, people will sometimes blame themselves for the loss and suffer with tormenting guilt. The cure for guilt is forgiveness.

Asking for and receiving forgiveness from God frees you from guilt. Focus on the beautiful gift of forgiveness instead of guilt. God will help you find peace in your heart. Whatever has already happened cannot be reversed. However, cling to the hope and promises of a better and brighter today and future.

The story of the "prodigal son" in the Holy Bible (Luke 15:11-32) is a parable that Jesus uses to teach people about how much how loves us; and opens His arms to them when we repent and turn from sin. We learn from this powerful lesson that God's response to our mistakes and imperfection doesn't involve reminding us about what is wrong. On the contrary, it illustrates God's compassion and love for us even when we turn away from Him. He celebrates when we return to His grace and He removes our guilt.

"If we confess our sins, he is faithful and just to forgive us our sins and to cleanse us from all unrighteousness."
—I John 1:9 (ESV)

Healing

"And He said to her, Daughter, your faith (your trust and confidence in Me, springing from faith in God) has restored you to health. Go in (into) peace and be continually healed and freed from your [distressing bodily] disease."
–Mark 5:34 (AMP)

As a child, I remember my great aunt, Bobbie saying, "God sits high, but looks low." I didn't quite understand the expression then, however today I do fully. God sees everything, especially our pain. And, it is His will that we are completely healed of our physical and emotional injuries.

As I have mentioned previously, God does not change life, He changes us. Sickness and loss in all of their forms can be healed. Divine healing generally works in two ways: God either removes the sickness from us or He removes us from the sickness.

Therefore, healing, restoration, and renewal will always take place. This should comfort us, particularly after loss. We must believe that God is a master doctor who has never lost a patient. We must voluntarily follow His prescription by trusting Him and not resisting His divine therapy for being whole.

"But He was wounded for our transgressions, He was bruised for our iniquities; the chastisement for our peace was upon Him, and by His stripes we are healed." — Isaiah 53:5 (NKJV)

Help Is Available 24/7

"I will lift up my eyes to the hills—from whence comes my help? My help *comes* from the Lord who made heaven and earth. He will not allow your foot to be moved; He who keeps you will not slumber." -Psalm 121: 1-3 (NKJV)

Problems don't disappear because we worry and/or fret about them. When we magnify our problems, they appear bigger. On the other hand, when we magnify God, our troubles become smaller. God promises that He will keep us. The Maker of heaven and earth also made a solution to every problem that exists. God never closes His eyes so that we can rest.

We can close our eyes because God's are open watching over us. We can sleep in peace because "He who keeps you will not slumber." He also said, "He will not allow your foot to be moved." In other words, our problems won't destroy us.

If we fall, we will rise again victoriously. Over the years, I have learned that trouble has the potential to draw us closer to God. In fact, the lessons gained through tribulation should make us wiser, stronger, and better in every dimension of our lives.

"Call to Me, and I will answer you, and show you great things, which you do not know." —Jeremiah 33:3 (NKJV)

His Pearl

"For we are God's handiwork, created in Christ Jesus to do good works, which God prepared in advance for us to do." — Ephesians 2:10 (NIV)

While most gemstones are buried deep within the earth's core, the pearl is found in a living organism, the oyster. The pearl is created during the biological process the oyster uses to protect itself from dangerous parasites and damaging debris.

When an invading irritant enters the pearl, it will work to protect itself by covering up the foreign particle with layers of nacre, the composite material that the oyster's mantle uses to create its shell. Thus, out of the oyster's trouble comes a beautiful object, the pearl.[1]

We, too, have infinite potential to create beautiful pearls. When we "cover" ourselves with hope, faith, charity, kindness, wisdom and most importantly, love to protect ourselves and others, we can transform our trials and troubles into priceless treasures.

At this very moment petition the Divine Creator of the Universe — God, to help you become His pearl and create the pearls in the world that you were born to manifest.

"For you formed my inward parts; you knitted me together in my mother's womb. I praise you, for I am fearfully and wonderfully made. Wonderful are your works; my soul knows it very well. My frame was not hidden from you, when I was being made in secret, intricately woven in the depths of the earth." — Psalm 139:13-15 (ESV)

Hope

"For I know the thoughts that I think toward you, says the LORD, thoughts of peace and not of evil, to give you a future and a hope." — Jeremiah 29:11 (NKJV)

Hope is painless, peaceful, risk-free, joyful, free, harmless, therapeutic, warming, encouraging, sustaining, and guiding. We lose absolutely nothing by putting our hope in Christ Jesus. Our life's beginning, middle and end becomes sweeter and sweeter when we hope in a Savior who is omnipotent, all-knowing, merciful, loving, compassionate, generous, forgiving, and kind.

Hope means that we believe that all things are possible. Hope lets us know that better days will replace the difficult ones. And, hope lets us laugh even when we feel like crying; it encourages us to hold on when we want to let go; and it builds our faith when fear is lurking and tries to steal our joy.

To build your hope, you must strengthen your faith. The first step is communicating with God, that is, you must talk to God about what's happening inside and around you. He already knows, but it pleases that you have faith in Him to resolve whatever issue you are facing.

Through prayer, you will get directives about what to do; when and how to complete whatever God commands. Hope in our Heavenly Father will change your perspective and transform your life. Believe.

"May the God of hope fill you with all joy and peace as you trust in him, so that you may overflow with hope by the power of the Holy Spirit." — Romans 15:13 (NIV)

Joy Comes in the Morning

"Weeping may endure for a night, but joy comes in the morning." — Psalm 30:5b (NKJV)

God is willing and able to heal your broken heart. He's like a master surgeon who takes out a malignant tumor in order to save your life. Always pray. God is listening and he deeply cares for you.

Whatever sadness you face today is only temporary. The dark clouds will be replaced with sunshine; your sorrow will be transformed into joy.

Never let yourself think that the presence of trouble equates the absence of God. In life you will have seasons of low moments, but God will lift you up in due season.

Stay hopeful; hold your head up and hang onto God's unchanging hand. He is there with you on the mountain and deep in the valley. Let yourself experience real joy by fine tuning your awareness of God's presence within and around you.

While joy doesn't always come instantly, it is experienced through nurturing our relationship with God. It is like a flower that blooms with water, sunshine and fertilizer.

Feed your faith and joy will grow and fill your garden with beauty, wisdom, peace, love, and vitality. Lastly, joy is a gift from God. It's an extension of God's compassion and love for us. It's up to us to accept it.

"Be joyful in hope, patient in affliction, faithful in prayer." — Romans 12:12 (NIV)

Kick Bad Habits

"Let all bitterness and wrath and anger and clamor and slander be put away from you, along with all malice. Be kind to one another, tenderhearted, forgiving one another, as God in Christ forgave you." -Ephesians 4:31-32 (ESV)

None of us is perfect. There are always one or more dimensions of our lives that need improvement. Facing the truth and taking action based on what is true will empower us to overcome and rise above obstacles. Kicking bad habits isn't easy but with God, all things are possible. We must lean on Him for support.

I know people who went through years of secular counseling to break bad habits, but it was only when they discovered the incomparable love of Jesus that the shackles of addiction were broken. God is real and He wants to heal us and make us whole. He has created us to be more than conquerors.

Our job is to surrender to His will and way — to trust in the power of His might. Simply put, we cannot do anything without Him. I can't take my next breath without the grace of God! Therefore, I certainly cannot kick destructive habits without His help. Try Jesus today and watch amazing things happen in your life.

"Remember not the former things, nor consider the things of old. Behold, I am doing a new thing; now it springs forth, do you not perceive it? I will make a way in the wilderness and rivers in the desert." — Isaiah 43:18-19 (ESV)

Love Comes from God

"Whoever does not love, does not know God, because God is love." —1 John 4:8 (NIV)

The cycle of people hurting people will continue until the end of time. Sometimes this is intentional but oftentimes it is not. Again, because people are imperfect, their relationships will never be. Pain, in some form or fashion is guaranteed, but it is not caused by love, but selfishness, the opposite of love.

It makes sense that we look to people for love because our presence on Earth is only made possible through people. We are not beamed from the sky like aliens depicted in science fiction movies. God designed humanity so that we would be interdependent upon people for the rest of our lives.

However, while our need to be loved, accepted and appreciated should come *through* people, the source of the supply can only come *from* God. Unfortunately, many people falsely believe that God is in some distant place, too far to be felt and heard. They don't understand that love is first an inner, spiritual experience before it is expressed outwardly in various forms. Moreover, many people only know God through books and religion. However, He is closer to us than anyone else. He will dwell in our hearts if we invite Him there. All real love comes from Him.

Meditate on this thought: human beings are not merely suffering because of their broken relationships with people; they are spiritually and emotionally deprived due to their lack of fellowship with God. In God's original blueprint for humanity, love was never meant to be excluded from relationships.

Love is a reflection of God's perfection and majesty; it must be the basis of all relationships. Through a relationship with God, you will experience the greatest love of all.

Love in Action

"But he who is greatest among you shall be your servant. And whoever exalts himself will be humbled, and he who humbles himself will be exalted."
–Jesus Christ (Matthew 23:11 NKJV)

While all of our blessings come *from* God, they are generally physically manifested *through* humans. It's rare that God uses rocks or trees to deliver His goodness; He generally uses people as instruments of His mind-blowing love. And, Our Creator doesn't discriminate; He chooses people with all shapes and sizes; all levels of education; all ethnic and racial backgrounds; and all social economic situations to do His will.

I will never forget the season in which I experienced unprecedented love in action in my personal life. It was a time when I was emotionally and financially devastated after a natural disaster. During this difficult time people demonstrated great love and compassion for me. Some of these people were complete strangers and others were people I had known almost my entire life, but had never expected such level of kindness from them. At the same time, there were people in my life who never offered me even a copper penny.

I am still humbled and awed by God's amazing grace and love. I now thank God for the flood because this event irreversibly changed my life in countless good ways. God helped me to discover that there are always beautiful treasures in every trial.

This life-changing event, gave me greater insight about myself, the people around me, and most importantly, the character of a loving and merciful God.

Love in Action

Among the many lessons, I discovered that you will never know who loves you until you need them. Whatever people **do** — their *actions* towards us ultimately indicate how much (or how little) we are loved by them. These actions are evidence of where we stand in people's lives. It is times of crisis that we learn how they see us. When people love us, it will inevitably show through their *deeds* because love inspires us to *do* for others. **"My little children, let us not love in word, neither in tongue; but in deed and in truth." (1 John 3:18 NKJV)**

Encouragement and prayer are empowering, and should never be dismissed or trivialized during times of suffering. However, when people are powerless to do for themselves, God requires that others demonstrate love through actions. When people are starving, they need food; when they are homeless, they need shelter and financial support; when they are hurting, they need empathy and compassion. This isn't always easy and cannot be done without great sacrifice and spiritual energy.

Love requires the highest level of selflessness. Only with God's divine help and inspiration can we possess the capacity to love others this way. Remember to study Jesus' life and emulate him as a model of this principle because as the author, Winn Collier stated, "Jesus not only proclaimed love. He lived love."

The high level of spiritual energy it takes to *act in love* explains why some of the people we think love us will not or cannot be there to pick us up when we fall. People might have good intentions but this isn't enough for God; He requires us to "do", not just talk and think about good. This doesn't mean that our blessings will be diminished or limited if people fall

Love in Action

short in this area of their lives. God will never fail to send the right people in our lives to meet our needs.

At the same time, people's failure to act with love should not become eternal indictments on their souls. If we are honest with ourselves, we will admit that we have been on both sides of this fence. In other words, we have failed to give when we should have. Therefore, we must not allow ourselves to become bitter if people disappoint us in times of trouble. God blesses us with both good and bad examples for a purpose. **We can use our own disappointment to become more conscientious and reflective people who work to rise above our weaknesses, failures and flaws and do the work of The Most High God.**

"What does it profit, my brethren, if someone says he has faith but does not have works? Can faith save him? If a brother or sister is naked and destitute of daily food and one of you says to them, depart in peace, be warmed and filled, but you do not give them the things which are needed for the body, what does it profit? Thus also faith by itself, if it does not have works, is dead. But someone will say, 'You have faith, and I have works.' Show me your faith without your works, and I will show you my faith by my works." (James 2:14-18 NKJV)

The truth is that it takes great spiritual work to be and remain selfless and give ourselves when it's not convenient and we face limited resources. In this chapter I share a few lessons I've learned the hard way about activating our faith and being vessels of God's love. I will be the first to admit that I have grossly failed at showing love when I needed to the most. Yet, I have learned that giving, even with limited resources, creates untold joy and blessings.

Love in Action

It is easy to talk, read and hear about God. However, to act as one of God's true representatives usually requires uncommon faith. As an ambassador of God's kingdom, we are mandated to sacrificially give our time and resources. This challenges us to strive for a higher level of selflessness that can only be achieved through fervent prayer, fasting and meditation.

Moreover, it requires that we not give due to our own human definitions of meritocracy. God desires that we put aside judgment, condemnation, and selectivity. **When God commands us to put our love in action there are no contingencies or conditions. We must give in spite of who people are and what they do. God desires that we cheerfully decide to give because of whom we represent — Him, the Author and Finisher of our faith.**

I personally know people who will pass one hundred homeless people to give to the rich. They dismiss the poor and downtrodden as cursed and unworthy of charity. They take from people who have nothing while lavishing themselves in luxury. They attend church every week and find scriptures to support their lifestyle of excessiveness and greed.

However, Jesus taught that we should feed the hungry; help strangers; clothe the naked; and visit people who are sick and imprisoned. He said, **"Assuredly, I say to you, inasmuch as you did to one of the least of these My brethren, you did it to Me." (Matthew 25:35-40 NKJV)**

Love in Action

The good news is that if we have life, we have an opportunity to change our attitudes and behavior. In fact, we cannot afford to remain selfish. For in that same chapter of Matthew, Jesus had a word for those who didn't help others. He said, **"Assuredly, I say to you inasmuch as you did not do it to one of the least of these, you did not do it to Me. And these [the people who refused to help] will go away into everlasting punishment, but the righteous into eternal life." (Matthew 25:45-46 NKJV)**

Keep in mind though that God doesn't expect us to attempt us to replace Him and become super humans. We will exhaust ourselves and even risk our health if we try to do more than what we are assigned to do. We cannot help every person we know.

The key is to respond to dire situations when people **need** our support. God will place people in our people in our path — in our circle of friends, whose circumstances give us an opportunity to demonstrate His love. God will convict us about what to do and when. We must not reject His voice.

Remember, our faith is nothing if we neglect to put love in action. **"What does it profit, my brethren, if someone says he has faith but does not have works? Can faith save him? If a brother or sister is naked and destitute of daily food and one of you says to them, depart in peace, be warmed and filled, but you do not give them the things which are needed for the body, what does it profit? Thus also faith by itself, if it does not have works, is dead. But someone will say, 'You have faith, and I have works.' Show me your faith without your works, and I will show you my faith by my works." (James 2:14-18 NKJV)**

Love in Action

Again, the key word is need. We must ask God every day to show us how we can meet the needs of others and be ambassadors of His love. Our actions might be grand or small; they might be noticed or done in secret. Our gifts might not always be monetary or tangible. Sometimes people need a non-judgmental and empathetic ear; sometimes people are encouraged by our smile and warm embrace. People also need our time and presence. All of us are called to be the salt and light of the Earth so **"let your light shine before men, that they may see your good words and glorify your Father in heaven." (Matthew 5:16 NKJV)**

To become a true agent of God's love is to reject notions of partiality, selectivity and favoritism. Who do we love? Only those who love us? Are we selective about who will receive our forgiveness, patience, tolerance, and longsuffering? If so, how can we truly represent God who **"makes His sun rise on the evil and on the good, and sends rain on the just and the unjust." (Matthew 5:45 NJKV)**

Assess your level of love in action. Seek God for wisdom and guidance on how you can strengthen your faith. There are countless ways we can show love. However, I address three specific issues because they often pose some of the greatest spiritual challenges to us.

Lesson One: Pray for people you know and those you don't.

The key to power is prayer. God is real and He hears everything we say to Him. It is imperative that you speak to God, not only about yourself and your beloved, but about the people around you. The people we think are the least deserving of our prayers are likely the people who need prayer the most.

Love in Action

We are not omnipotent and omnipresent, but God is. He can do what is humanly impossible for us. He responds to sincere, desperate and heartfelt intercessory prayer. He honors the prayers of the righteous. Sacrifice time to ask Him to meet the needs of people—all people, the good, the bad, and the ugly.

Again, don't be selective about the subject of your prayers. Some people are so sick, lost and hurting that they cannot or will not even pray for themselves. They need you to intercede on their behalf. If you are as I am, you were saved from death because people lifted you up in prayer.

At the same time, don't let prayer be your only action. Pray and *do* for others. This is how we show we are the true sons and daughters of a loving God. Give to people whether the gift is big or small.

Scripture: "**And the prayer of faith will save the sick, and the Lord will raise him up. And if he has committed sins, he will be forgiven. Confess your trespasses to one another, and pray for one another, that you may be healed. The effective, fervent prayer of a righteous man avails much.**" **(James 5:16 NKJV)**

Lesson Two: Cheerfully give without judgment; without conditions and contingencies.

Mother Teresa once said, "When you love people, you have no time to judge them." We cannot just give to people who we feel merit our charity. I know people who see others at their lowest point and they will say, "I'm not giving because…" However, when Jesus taught his disciples about giving, He never gave specific criteria about who should receive what, how and when. His command was simple:

Love in Action

"Give and it shall be given to you: good measure, pressed down, shaken together, and running over will be put into your bosom. For with the same measure that you use, it will be measured back to you." (Luke 6:38 NKJV)

I often teach young people that we do not get what we want; we get what we give. Our lives are like gardens. Whatever we plant is the only thing that will grow. If I plant tomato seeds, I will not get pumpkins. I will not get lemons if I plant orange seeds. This law is true and unchangeable from a natural and supernatural perspective. I personally believe that whatever we want in life, we must first give it. If I want respect, I give it. If I want love, I must first plant it in the universe.

Many people are miserable because of unrequited dreams and desires. They remain in a chronic state of frustration because what they want seems to evade them. Yet, while they want love, they give hate. They want to be rich, but they will not give a copper penny to people in need. They want respect and compassion, but they have none for other people. They ask for the truth but they live a life of deception.

I have learned that whenever I feel disappointed to seek out the lesson that God is trying to teach me. So often, I have failed to do the very thing I wanted for myself. God pricks my heart and reminds me of the law of the harvest. I will not get what I haven't sown. At the same time, I cannot give just to get. God is not like a soda machine: we don't put something in and expect what we want to instantly appear.

Whenever we give, it must be motivated by love. Our actions are mirrors of God's love flowing through us. While we can give without love; we cannot love without giving. When the love of God is in us, we give cheerfully expecting nothing in return. When God has been merciful and kind to

Love in Action

us, we cannot stop ourselves from giving. Giving becomes an involuntary action that we do naturally like breathing.

Some people believe that when people suffer that God is punishing them. They falsely believe that this justifies withholding their blessings. However, Jesus instructed us to **"Give to everyone who asks of you. And from him who takes away your goods do not ask them back. And just as you want men to do to you, you also do to them likewise... But love your enemies, do good and lend, hoping for nothing in return; and your reward will be great, and you will be sons of the Most High for He is kind to the unthankful and evil. Therefore be merciful as your Father also is merciful. Judge not and you shall not be judged. Condemn not, and you shall not be condemned. Forgive and you shall be forgiven." (Luke 6:30-37 NKJV)**

Wow! God wants us to emulate Him with our actions. He loves and gives to all and we must do the same. **Giving becomes easier when you deal with what is in your heart.** Again, giving without love and the genuine desire to do so is not pleasing to God. Whenever giving becomes a struggle, we must ask God to transform our hearts. What is in our heart ultimately determines what we will do. The lack of giving is not due to an empty bank account, but a heart that is devoid of God's love.

Scripture: "Create in me a clean heart, O God. And renew a steadfast spirit within me. Do not cast me away from Your presence. And do not take Your Holy Spirit from me. Restore to me the joy of Your salvation. And uphold me to Your generous Spirit. Then I will teach transgressors Your ways. And sinners shall be converted to You." (Psalm 51:10-13 NJKV)

Love in Action

Lesson Three: Accept people as they are.

Some people might find it interesting that throughout the history of mankind, God chose to use people from all walks of life to do His work. He didn't let a person's socioeconomic status, race, education, gender, imperfection, health, past, or even level of faith disqualifies him/her from being His ambassador. There is so much work to be done in God's kingdom. God is looking for people who will trust Him and *act* on their faith.

On the other hand, humans often categorize people based on superficial factors. When we reject people because of our biases we are doing the opposite of what God does — accept people as they are. Only God has the power to transform people, but we have the power to inspire people to change. We can only do this when we accept and treat them with respect and love. While we can reject bad behavior, we must not reject the person.

This might be difficult, but it is possible to achieve. Personally, I believe it's easier when you see others as yourself. I simply cannot afford to give to people what I need for myself. I need patience, tolerance, forgiveness, etc. from others so I recognize the joy of "paying it forward." No, this doesn't always happen instantaneously, but if God is truly in our hearts, there is no way we can reject the people that He accepts.

Even if we cannot have relationships with every person we meet, being rude, mean and disrespectful is never justified. We are not responsible for what other people do. However, God will hold us responsible for how we respond to people — even the unkind and negative. We will all have to give an account for everything we have said and done. **I am not**

Love in Action

suggesting that we should allow ourselves to be punching bags and dartboards for toxic people. The point is that we cannot do wrong just because other people do.

The God we serve is "gracious and full of compassion. Slow to anger and great in mercy. The Lord is good to all. And His tender mercies are all His works." (Psalm 145:8-9 NKJV) Throughout the gospels, Jesus taught that we should act on our faith by any means necessary. In other words, we must do what is right regardless of the circumstances. God doesn't strike people down when they do wrong. In fact, He doesn't want to destroy humans. He wants to save them.

Here is what Jesus said to His disciples: "A new commandment I give to you, that you love one another as I have loved you, that you also love one another. By this all will know that you are My disciples if you have love for one another."(John 13:34-35 NKJV)

If Jesus loved people who forsook Him; denied Him; rejected Him; and worked to destroy Him, can we not love also? He put love into action by focusing on God's love, not people's shortcomings. Because He depended upon God for strength, He prayed for, blessed and sacrificed His life for those who rejected Him. If we are our Heavenly Father's children, we have inherited His character. We can love as He does because we belong to Him.

Reflect on the following sayings: (1) "actions speak louder than words"; (2) "a sermon seen is far more effective than one said"; (3) "you may be the only Bible a person will ever read". Assess the ways you demonstrate the love of God to others. Do you help people when they ask for it or do you make excuses? Have you forgiven those who hurt you or are you holding grudges?

Love in Action

In conclusion, all of us must ask God to help us be a reflection of His character and love with our actions. The truth is that we cannot do this within our own strength. He will help us give to others what He has given us — grace, compassion, mercy, peace, joy, love...

Love Your Children Unconditionally

"Fathers, do not provoke your children to anger, but bring them up in the discipline and instruction of the Lord."
–Ephesians 6:4 (ESV)

Children who know they are loved are generally better behaved than those who don't feel that way. Love is the most essential ingredient to feeling confident and valued. Love your children when they do good things; love them when they do bad things.

Love your children when they make you proud; love them when they disappointment you. Love them when they succeed; love them when they fail. Tell your children you love them every chance you get. Let them know you must discipline them and teach them character because you love them.

When love is the guiding force for all of your actions as a mother, you will significantly reduce discipline problems in your home. Continually nurture your relationship with God, the ultimate source of love. You will create a priceless legacy that future generations of children will honor.

"[Your] children will not remember you for the material thing you provided but for the feeling that you cherished them." –Richard L. Evans

As an educator for almost 30 years I have seen the very best and worst of behavior. Parents who have unconditional love for their children see problems as teachable moments. They generally have better outcomes than those who are abusive, reactionary, and explosive.

Children need adults who can assist them with working through their problems with love and patience.

Love Your Children Unconditionally

Condemnation, criticism, and violence do not work. They are ineffective ways for improving behavior. These destructive forms of discipline hinder children rather than help them. Measure the effectiveness of your discipline techniques by what you observe. Do you see improvement or is the situation getting worse? Remember, it makes no sense to do something that doesn't create favorable results.

As always, seek God's wisdom and power when choosing the best forms of discipline for your beloved children. He is the best Counselor for tailor-made techniques that will perfectly fit every child according to his or her needs. Keep in mind that when love permeates in a home, the less discipline problems will exist. God's unfailing love prevents resentment, anger, sibling rivalry, favoritism, un-forgiveness, hypocrisy and discord. Therefore, let love be the first strategy for effective discipline. More love means less behavior issues.

"Behold, children are a heritage from the Lord, the fruit of the womb a reward." –Psalm 127:3 (ESV)

Mercy versus Meritocracy: Doing Things God's Way

"And they did not receive him, because his face was as though he would go to Jerusalem. And when his disciples James and John saw this, they said, 'Lord, wilt thou that we command fire to come down from heaven, and consume them, even as Elias did?' But he turned, and rebuked them, and said, 'Ye know not what manner of spirit ye are of. For the Son of man is not come to destroy men's lives, but to save them.' And they went to another village." -Luke 9:53-55 (KJV)

According to a biblical account in the book of Luke, when the Samaritans did not welcome Jesus in their city, the disciples wanted them destroyed. Jesus, on the other hand, reminded the disciples that He came to the world to save lives, not to destroy them. God is swift to show mercy while man is swifter to cast harsh judgment based on his perceptions of merit.

In the disciples' minds, the Samaritans *deserved* the ultimate penalty of death because of what they *did*. However, if we claim to be followers of Christ, we must emulate His example. We must be merciful to both kind and unkind people; accomplished and unaccomplished; and the strong as well as the weak.

Imagine a man standing before you and God. His spiritual résumé doesn't look impressive. Would you give him a second chance? God wouldn't withhold His goodness based on merit, so as His children we must demonstrate the same behaviour.

Mercy versus Meritocracy: Doing Things God's Way

God looks beyond our faults, weaknesses and transgressions and blesses us anyway. Meritocracy is a part of the world's system which gives according to its ideas of value and achievement. With God, your worth is not measured by what you *can* do, but who you are—His child!

"For the LORD *is* good; his mercy *is* everlasting; and his truth *endureth* to all generations." –Psalm 100:5 (KJV)

Mothers Should Lead by Example

"Psychologists will attest that parents can program their children for joy and achievement with the words they share and the example they set." -Angela Burt-Murray

When I was around fourteen years old, I watched my mother graduate from college with honors. After giving birth to four children, she made a decision to complete the post-secondary education she had started before I was born. I remember this being one of the proudest moments of my childhood.

Today I realize my mother's powerful example of returning to school, even against the odds, inspired me to endure my own difficult college days. My mother modelled for my sisters and me, not only the value of getting an education, but also the importance of finishing what you start, as well as, how hard work pays off. I believe in my heart that my mother's example of resilience and perseverance attributed to all four of her children becoming college graduates.

To be effective mothers, we don't have to be perfect. However, we should do everything in our power to give our children a model of how to live with integrity in spite of our imperfections and mistakes. **As mothers, we are our children's first and most influential teachers.** Our children are constantly observing our behaviour even when we think they are not; they will subconsciously emulate our conduct even if we try to convince them not to. As mothers, we need to be our best so that our children can be. They benefit from our good choices, but suffer and become casualties of unrighteous living.

"He who walks with the wise grows wise, but a companion of fools suffers harm." –Proverbs 13:20 (NIV)

Mothers Should Lead by Example

A mother is truly the heart of her family. She creates the ambience of her home. Her decisions, thoughts and values as well as words, directly impact her children's behaviour. To operate as an honorable mother, she cannot neglect investing in the resources that will nurture her mind, body and spirit. She must also be willing to admit her shortcomings and adjust her behaviour if necessary to enhance the health of her family. This will teach children how to take ownership of their mistakes.

Unfortunately, some women believe that motherhood is synonymous with "making children behave". They attempt to do this by constantly barking out directives and criticizing children when they make mistakes. However, domination and control are adversaries of righteous parenting.

Effective parenting involves teaching "how to", which involves good examples, not just telling your children what to do. In other words, mothers must be willing model the same behavior they expect from their children.
A good mother inculcates values which come from God. Later, through her actions, she becomes a living example of how to implement and practice the lessons she taught. It is evitable though that all mothers will make mistakes. However, a mother's mistakes can be used to teach powerful lessons about recovery and correction.

"The wise woman builds her house,
 but with her own hands the foolish one tears hers down."- Proverbs 14:1 (NIV)

Pain, the Great Teacher

"It is good for me that I have been afflicted; that I might learn your statutes." –Psalm 119:71 (NKJV)

When I was much younger, I didn't have the healthy view of God that I do today. I used to think that God was some great power in the sky that kept tabs on everything I did wrong. Whenever I was going through difficulty, I thought God is punishing me for something. While some of our suffering is a result of consequences from poor decisions, that's not the only reason we must endure painful experiences.

As a mature believer, I now understand that **God doesn't change life, He changes us**. All humans go through a variation of the same problems and even with a relationship with God, some pain is inevitable. However, the outcome for believers is that God works everything out for our good.

God never wastes our pain and uses it to make us stronger, wiser and more grateful. Through pleasant and uncomfortable times we should praise God for His goodness. **We must pray that God gives us clarity to grasp the powerful spiritual lessons that sometimes we can only learn through pain.** We can rejoice that our tears won't last forever. In the end, joy comes and we are better than we were before. **Glory be to our loving Heavenly Father who knows how to use our pain for a purpose.**

"Pain is the best instructor but no one wants to go to his class." –Choi Hong Hi

Perfect Peace

"You will keep in perfect peace all those who trust in you, all whose thoughts are fixed on you!" –Isaiah 26:3 (NLT)

At some point most of us learn that everyday problems can rob us of our peace and joy. While it is imperative that we work to be responsible, law-abiding and blameless, we cannot avoid certain challenges, no matter how hard we try. The good news is that we can still have incredible peace in the midst of trouble if we keep our mind on God. In fact, the more we meditate on God and His power, the smaller our problems appear.

On the other hand, focusing on what's wrong only seems to exacerbate things. We can potentially become more depressed and hopeless. We must never forget that we have the ability to change what we mentally focus on. We can ruminate about problems we cannot solve or we can trust God and keep our thoughts fixed on Him.

The remote control is in our hands: all we have to do is change the channel to GPP (God's Perfect Plan). That is when we will discover that everything we are going through is preparing us for bigger and better blessings in the future.

True peace is not the absence of tribulation; it's knowing that God is always with us. He carries us through our trials and shows us the lessons in it all. In the end, all things will work out for our good. We must have faith and believe.

"Casting all your anxieties on him, because he cares for you." —I Peter 5:7 (ESV)

Pray Until Something Happens

In Luke 18: 1-8, Jesus uses a parable to teach people that they "always ought to pray and not lose heart." (v.1) This insightful story used to help believers understand God's faithfulness involves a widow repeatedly going to a judge who fears neither man nor God.

The judge doesn't respond to the woman's request at first, but eventually He does what she asks because of her resilience in petitioning Him. Jesus reminds us that God will do more for His children "who cry out day and night to Him" (v. 7). Therefore, it is imperative that no matter how big or small our request is to God, we must make it known until He answers us.

God is concerned about justice, and while mankind's doesn't always prevail in our favor, God's will. He will avenge the innocent and those who are persecuted without a cause. As Jesus said, don't lose heart. Pray until you see something happen!

"Don't worry about anything; instead, pray about everything. Tell God what you need, and thank him for all he has done. Then you will experience God's peace, which exceeds anything we can understand. His peace will guard your hearts and minds as you live in Christ Jesus."
–Philippians 4:6-7 (NLT)

Quit Blaming Others

"Do not be conformed to this world, but be transformed by the renewal of your mind, that by testing you may discern what is good and acceptable and perfect."
—Romans 12:2 (ESV)

This used to be one of my favorite pastimes. I wanted people to feel ashamed and guilty for hurting me. I wanted them punished for the various forms of abuse I suffered. I would constantly talk about other people's faults. I was attempting to uncover their evil, but I forgot how God covered my own faults with His love.

One day I had a terrible repressed memory. I thought about how God had been so kind and merciful to me. I was reminded how He repeatedly covered my sins. I recalled how He did not let me die during my darkest moments of brokenness.

As I prayed (mainly complained) about my pain to God, He revealed to me that I was just as guilty as the people who hurt me. I was no different than they were if I continued to accuse and judge them. I was literally shaken with conviction to stop blaming other people for my problems. God showed me that nothing happened to me that He did not allow. My pain had a purpose. I decided from that moment forth, that I would create a hundred moments of joy, for every tear I had ever shed.

I suddenly understood that the road to my *vocation*, teaching, was not a result of happenstance. My experiences were attached to my destiny. They had prepared me to empower young people to maximize their potential; to not let disadvantages and distractions stop them from being successful. I thanked God for changing my heart and

Quit Blaming Others

reframing my thoughts. The more I thanked Him, the more painful memories He erased from the ebbs of my mind. Say this three times: "I will no longer blame others for my pain."

When you take ownership of your thoughts and feelings, you are no longer weak and powerless to accomplish great things. You transcend from victim to victor when you determine that no one determines your destiny but God. Although you can't control every experience that occurs in your life, you can choose your responses to them.

As Joyce Meyer once said, "You can either be powerful or pitiful, but you can't be both." Make a choice not to succumb to the agony of someone defeating you—someone else determining if you can be happy or sad. Decide that you will liberate yourself from other people's domination over you.

Reconcile

"If it is possible, as much as it depends on you, live peaceably with all men." — Romans 12:18 (NKJV)

For some people it is easier to hear and/or read about a miracle than it is to see and experience one up close and personal. Reconciliation, particularly after a tumultuous experience, is a miracle from God. The biblical stories of Joseph and his brothers (Genesis 37-45) and the prodigal son and his father (Luke 15:11-32) are just a few ancient examples of recorded acts of reconciliation in the Holy Bible.

However, the newspapers are filled with modern-day stories of reconciliation such as Mary Johnson who forgave and reconciled with her son's killer, Oshea Israel. Also, a well-known evangelist, Joyce Meyer often talks about forgiving and reconciling with the father who sexually abused her.

There are also thousands of stories (past and present) of men and women reconciling with God. One notable bible story is about what happened to King David after he sinned against God with Bathsheba. (2 Samuel 11) I cannot count the number of times that I have heard of people living their lives in darkness, but finally surrendered to the power of God's love.

Reconciliation is only possible through God's grace. It takes an enormous amount of spiritual energy. Most of the time, it never happens because it is dependent upon work from both (or all) people involved with tumultuous situation. Forgiveness can be done by a single person but reconciliation (re-establishing a relationship with someone who intentionally hurt you or a loved one) takes cooperative effort.

Reconcile

When we pray for people who hurt us—and forgive them, God will move on our behalf. Sometimes, it is His will that people restore broken relationships. He will use reconciliation for His glory and purpose. I am blessed to personally know the depth of God's desire to heal broken unions and reunite lost loved ones. If He did it for me, He will do it for you. Ask God for reconciliation if it is your desire.

Reflections on Motherhood

"Every wise woman buildeth her house, but the foolish plucketh it down with her hands." –Proverbs 14:1 (KJV)

First, let me say that children don't need a mother, they need a righteous mother. While motherhood is an honorable gift from God, it requires a high level of personal responsibility and accountability. Whatever a mother does, says, and thinks will directly or indirectly affect her children.

Therefore, it is imperative that a mother becomes self-reflective. She must be willing to make adjustments to her own behavior and environment in order to provide for, protect, teach and nurture her children. Throughout history notable people have credited their mothers with giving them the tools to be successful.

The following are just a few actions you can take to become a more effective mother; one that your children will cherish, honor and respect. (More detailed lessons can be found in *Wise and Wonderful: Life Lessons for Single Mothers*)

1. Love your children unconditionally
2. Watch and pray
3. Take care of yourself
4. Lead by example
5. Build healthy relationships with your children
6. Communicate blessings, not curses
7. Emphasize potential, not problems
8. Discipline with love
9. Take one day at a time
10. Trust God for His provisions
11. Accept that living without a man won't damage your children
12. Let go and let God
13. Work to heal broken relationships

Reflections on Motherhood

Finally, I encourage you to establish and/or strengthen your relationship with God which allows you to see your children as blessings, not burdens. God's amazing grace, love and wisdom will make your legacy as a mother honorable. Don't just pray about your children, pray about yourself. Ask God to show you how to be a good steward over the children He has gifted to you. Trust in Him, and you will not fail!

"Favour is deceitful, and beauty is vain: but a woman that feareth the Lord, she shall be praised." –Proverbs 31:31 (KJV)

Rest in His Arms

"Come unto me all you who labor and heavy laden, and I will give you rest." — Matthew 11:28 (NKJV)

    During moments of great suffering we discover that God is a source of divine comfort and power. While things and people must die in our lives, God is the Eternal One. He will never leave us.

    He will carry us in His bosom during loss and replace joy for our sorrow; light for the darkness; peace for our worry; and love for selfishness. Loss forces us to yield to this God. It helps us to trust in Him. When the weeping subsides and the quiet begins to bud in our hearts, we will get to know Him for ourselves.

    Our fellowship nurtures an intimacy unlike anything we know. It is spiritual and supernatural, not born of the flesh. It is incomparable to any human relationship. Today, let God show you just how much He loves you. He has been waiting to envelop you with His amazing grace. Do not reject Him.

    Do not think that He loves you less because He allowed loss to occur in your life. He wants to teach you something that you can only learn when He removes things and people from your life.

Speak with Love, Not Criticism

"Do not let any unwholesome talk come out of your mouths, but only what is helpful for building others up according to their needs, that it may benefit those who listen."
— Ephesians 4:29 (NIV)

Criticism is a totally ineffective way to help people improve their lives. History has taught us that it doesn't work. Simply put, people rarely do better as a result of criticism. In fact, it often discourages people and creates an emotional downward spiral which reinforces problems. In my experiences as an educator and parent, focusing on the solutions and presenting them in a way that demonstrates genuine care usually produces better behavioural outcomes.

Most people can point out people's faults because it is the easiest response to situations. On the other hand, it takes much more spiritual energy, compassion, and most importantly, unconditional love to inspire people to constructively transform their lives. I believe it is paramount that we ask our Heavenly Father to anoint and appoint us before offering counsel.

It is the Holy Spirit (not our human power or personality) that allows people to receive a righteous message in the first place. It is God, working through us, that helps us to effectively encourage people to direct their attention to Him, our divine problem-solver rather than their problems. Additionally, it's important to speak and promote what we believe is His truth without condemnation of others.

In fact, I believe we should not waste time lamenting about what is wrong. Instead, we should teach, by example first, what we know is right. The most important lesson we

Speak with Love, Not Criticism

can share is that we can do nothing without wisdom, power and strength from the LORD. Because of Him, we are more than conquerors!

"Do everything without grumbling or arguing, so that you may become blameless and pure, 'children of God without fault in a warped and crooked generation'. Then you will shine among them like stars in the sky as you hold firmly to the word of life." — Philippians 2:14-16a

Stay in the Race!

> "I have fought the good fight, I have finished the race, I have kept the faith. Now there is in store for me the crown of righteousness, which the Lord, the righteous Judge, will award to me on that day—and not only to me, but also to all who have longed for his appearing."
> -II Timothy 4:7-8 (NIV)

I am not much of a sports enthusiast, but every blue moon I will watch a culminating athletic event like the Super Bowl or the French Open. It still amazes me how the men and women who play these sports demonstrate uncommon physical prowess and strength as they represent the best in their fields. Behind their Olympian stature is one goal: to win—to be crowned as number one, second to none!

As people of faith, however, winning is not about being better than anyone else. It's about staying connected to God and finishing our personal race according to what He has predestined for us. In other words, it's about completion, not competition. We must not look to the left or right, but look up to our faithful God who guides us. In fact, it's exhausting trying to outdo our neighbours.

Moreover, competition sabotages love. Remember, our faith is about God's victory since our battles really belong to Him. He is the true victor. He simply works through us to accomplish His will. He uses us as vessels to manifest kingdom-work. Be encouraged to engage in the "good fight" of faith.

Do your best and let God deal with the rest. Life with Him isn't about *being* first, it's about putting Him first. Reflect on Jesus' words: "…but whoever desires to become great

Stay in the Race!

among you, let him be your servant. And whoever desires to be first among you, let him be your slave." -Matthew 20:26b-27 (NKJV)

You see, there are no trophies to be won and special titles to be gained. Winning is about serving others and at times being last so people can have their physical and spiritual needs met. Just let your faith be your Gatorade and stay in the game of life! With Jesus as your cheerleader, you will not fail. Victory is inevitable.

"I have observed something else under the sun. The fastest runner doesn't always win the race, and the strongest warrior doesn't always win the battle. The wise sometimes go hungry, and the skillful are not necessarily wealthy. And those who are educated don't always lead successful lives. It is all decided by chance, by being in the right place at the right time." -Ecclesiastes 9:11 (NLT)

Strength

"He gives power to the weak, and to those who have no might He increases strength."-Isaiah 40:29 (NKJV)

    During difficult times, our pain can seem unbearable. However, we can tap into an endless supply of strength from God. God's strength cannot be explained and rationalized by our finite human minds. It is a miracle, a preternatural phenomenon that can only be understood by using the spiritual dimension of ourselves.

    We can be confident that God's everlasting strength will always compensate for our weaknesses, our infirmities, and our human fragility. The truth is that we can do nothing without it. We need it to triumph over our trials and tribulations.

    God's strength empowers us to rise each morning knowing that our hearts are aching; it gives us the courage to face our fears. His strength allows us to transform our thoughts and find good, understanding, and hope, even in painful circumstances. God welcomes us to lean on Him and use His strength to do amazing things.

    "So do not fear, for I am with you; do not be dismayed, for I am your God. I will strengthen you and help you; I will uphold you with my righteous right hand." — Isaiah 41:10 (NIV)

    "God is our refuge and our strength, an ever-present help in trouble." -Psalm 46:3 (NIV)

Supernatural Transformative Power

The writers of the gospel according to Mark chronicle a story of after Jesus giving a crowd spiritual food. He also takes five loaves of bread and two fish to feed thousands of people. There are some powerful principles from this story that we all can incorporate in our own lives today. Below are some lessons to reflect upon. (Mark 6: 31-44 NKJV)

We must demonstrate compassion. Jesus was compassionate. "And Jesus, when He came out, saw a great multitude and was moved with compassion for them because they were like sheep not having a shepherd." (Mark 6:34) If you follow the entire story, you will find that the disciples wanted to send the crowd away after a long day of learning with Jesus. Jesus, on the other hand, wanted to make sure that they had eaten before they left his presence (Mark 6: 37) Daily we must ask God for the strength and wisdom to serve people regardless of the circumstances.

We must follow God's commands. Jesus told the people to sit down in groups and they did. (Mark 6:39) God is continually giving us directives about what to do, when and how to do it. We must be careful, not just to listen, but to do what He says. When we trust in Him, we will never be disappointed. God's glory is manifested *through* us when we are obedient.

We must give what we have. God doesn't ask us to give what we don't have — that's His job. God is omniscient and knows everything about us, including what we have. He is able to take a little and supernaturally multiply it when we are working to help people. God is faithful to provide all that we need.

Supernatural Transformative Power

We must look to heaven, bless what God has given us, and share with others. According to Mark 6:41, that is exactly what Jesus did. The Bible teaches that "they all ate and were filled." They even had leftovers! (Mark 6:42-43) Each of us has the commission to share our blessings. God's adds to our lives when we subtract what we have. This allows us to inspire and empower the people around us.

God's supernatural transformative power can never be extinguished. God wants to use us to do great work for His kingdom. When we follow His roadmap and guidance, we will never get lost. With Him our destiny involves efficacy and abundance.

"Search me, O God, and know my heart: try me, and know my thoughts: And see if there be any wicked way in me, and lead me in the way everlasting."-Psalm 139:23-24 (KJV)

Talk to God about Your Children

"Do not be anxious about anything, but in everything by prayer and supplication with thanksgiving let your requests be made known to God." — Philippians 4:6 (ESV)

Being an effective mother involves much more than getting children to meet our personal expectations and making them do what *we* want. One of the most important roles of a parent is to build character. It is ultimately character that will protect our children from unnecessary disappointment and hardship. Character allows them to keep what they earn throughout their lives; it helps them use the natural gifts endowed by God in ways that benefit mankind.

Therefore, it is paramount that as mothers we watch and fervently pray for our children without ceasing. Moreover, we must let God's plans guide us on what values to inculcate in our children — which lessons to teach that will save them rather than those that cause unnecessary pain, suffering, and pre-mature death. This can be quite difficult for mothers who are parenting alone. The parenting techniques that are the quickest and easiest are generally not the most useful for shaping children with good character.

However, talking to God about our children is one of the most effective parenting strategies that we can employ. After all, our children come from Him. It is imperative that we consult Him on a regular basis about what's best for them. It is God who has placed children in our stewardship.

Therefore, we need to seek Him out because He knows our children better than anyone. He is the Divine Manufacturer and Creator of all things. It is He who wired each child with his/her inherent gifts, personality, and

Talk to God about Your Children

physical attributes, just as He made us, the mothers charged with tenderly caring for His property.

God is the best person to talk to (pray) about what is happening in our children's lives because His omniscience allows Him to see things about them that we don't and cannot. If we submit to God's authority, He will guide us and equip us with the tools to prepare our children for His purpose.

That's What I'm Made For

"Continue earnestly in prayer, being vigilant in it with thanksgiving." -Colossians 4:2 (NKJV)

Not long ago, a friend was encouraging me. We both talked about the power of intercessory prayer and how blessed we felt to know we are (and were) benefactors of it. I was moved when he said that he'd pray for me, followed by, *"That's what I'm made for."*

That simple, yet profound statement resonated with me throughout the evening. We are indeed made to pray for one another. No matter how busy we are; and no matter how dismal the circumstances might appear, we must fervently pray for God's perfect will to be done and that we have the grace and knowledge to accept and fulfill His will.

Below are a few of many scriptures that remind us of the importance of praying for our friends — and even our enemies. All scriptures are taken from the English Standard Version of the Holy Bible.

"But I say to you, Love your enemies and pray for those who persecute you." -Matthew 5:44

"Praying at all times in the Spirit, with all prayer and supplication. To that end keep alert with all perseverance, making supplication for all the saints." -Ephesians 6:18

"First of all, then, I urge that supplications, prayers, intercessions, and thanksgivings be made for all people," -I Timothy 2:1

The Balanced Life

"To everything there is a season, a time for every purpose under the heaven." — Ecclesiastes 3:1(NKJV)

It's easy to get so busy in this fast-paced society that we fail to create a life of harmony and balance for ourselves and those around us. It isn't difficult to become distracted by the billion things that are happening in the world that we lose perspective of what should be a priority versus an option; what should be first or dead-last; and what is meaningful instead of trivial.

The key to a balanced life is to put God first. He should be first on our minds in the morning and the last one we think about before going to sleep. Why? Without God our lives have no direction. It is only through a personal and deep relationship with Him that we can **avoid** becoming mindless, nomads moving about life without a true sense of purpose and belonging.

Our Heavenly Father wants us to experience all that He has created for us to the fullest extent. It grieves His heart that we give our attention to everything and everyone, but Him. He longs to fellowship with us while an imbalanced life plagues us with the nagging feeling that something is missing. And, only God, the author and finisher of our faith can heal us and make our lives feel complete with all that we need. Therefore, we must seek His face above all others, and our lives will have the order and balance we need to be fruitful and complete our divine assignments.

When we accept that God is more important than anything else, we stay focused; maintain the right attitude, even through troublesome times and still get the kingdom

The Balanced Life

work done. This is because enjoying a life of balance means that God is the center of our attention.

When we work, play, study, create and give, we should do so with God in our hearts. The by-products of a God-centered life are balance and peace. These then lead to countless more blessings including health, prosperity and significance.

On the other hand, unrest (both physical and spiritual), however is a result of being entangled in the traps of the world such as giving our time and attention to unwholesome things and doing useless things too much while neglecting to do what is empowering and necessary to fulfil God's will. This imbalance causes us to feel overly weary and frustrated. Furthermore, it makes us impotent to honor God with our thoughts, words and deeds.

Meditate on the following several scriptures to start creating a life of balance for you and your family.

"Seek first the Kingdom of God above all else, and live righteously, and he will give you everything you need." — Matthew 6:33 (NLT)

"For with God, nothing will be impossible." — Luke 1:37 (NKJV)

"The thief cometh not, but for to steal, and to kill, and to destroy: I am come that they might have life, and they might have it more abundantly." — John 10:10 (KJV)

"So Jesus said to them, 'Because of your unbelief; for assuredly, I say to you, if you have faith as a mustard seed, you will say to this mountain, 'Move from here to there,' and it will move; and nothing will be impossible for you."

-Matthew 17:20 (NKJV)

The Balanced Life

"You adulterous people, don't you know that friendship with the world means enmity against God? Therefore, anyone who chooses to be a friend of the world become an enemy of God." —James 4:4 (NIV)

The First Step

"Your word is a lamp for my feet, a light on my path."
—Psalm 119:105 (NIV)

The biggest act of faith involves taking the first step. I cannot tell you how amazing things happen when you take a step of faith towards your purpose. Faith pleases God. Throughout history we have been left with accounts of people who took actions to complete tasks that couldn't be accomplished with mere human capital. These faithful men and women didn't have to know all the answers upfront; they didn't have to trust themselves and their own ability.

Models of faith, past and present, move based on their trust in God. They know (without a hint of doubt) that God will neither leave nor forsake them, so they take actions to complete a God-inspired task without having all of the specific details of the outcomes. People of faith just know that God will manifest His power THROUGH them when they lean of Him.

You don't have to know all the intricate details of a situation and the outcome. When you trust God and you know without a shadow of doubt that He loves you, you will move forward with the plans that God has put in your heart. As I heard someone once say, "We are responsible for the effort [and the first step], God is responsible for the final outcome."

When God is directing our steps, we will never end up in the wrong place. We can do what seems like a daunting task, not due to our own might, but because our God is mightier than anything or anyone else.

The Last 12 Words of Jesus Christ

"I am with you always, even to the end of the age."
–Matthew 28:20b (NKJV)

As we commemorate the resurrection of our Lord and Savior, Jesus Christ, let us remember some of his most powerful words. Jesus spent most of his short, adult life praying; healing people; and teaching others how to have a relationship with God, and with mankind.

Jesus Christ is the ultimate example for how we should live, as well as, what we should think and say. We are blessed to have a record of how Jesus modeled righteous behavior. The semi-biographical record of his life can be found mainly in the four gospels (Matthew, Mark, Luke and John) of the Holy Bible.

The lessons written thousands of years ago are still relative today. They are the most transformative and empowering ever discovered. Keep in mind, too that according to John 19:30 and John 21:25, everything Jesus did could not be contained in books.

The following are just a few of the countless lessons Jesus taught. Let us inculcate them in our hearts.

Prayer is the key to power. (Matthew 6:5; Matthew 6:5-13; Matthew 14:23; Matthew 17:21; Matthew 21:22; Matthew 26:41; Mark 1:35; Mark 11:24; Luke 6:12; John 17:9)

Forgiveness is essential to please God and have peace. (Matthew 6:14-15; Matthew 18:35; Luke 7; Luke 11:16-34; John 20:23)

Love is a commandment from God. (Matthew 5:43-44; Matthew 22:37-40; John 15:12-13, 17)

The Last 12 Words of Jesus Christ

Focus on God, not the things of this world. (Matthew 6:19-34; Matthew 7:3-14; Matthew 10:28; Matthew 13:31-32; Matthew 18:7-9; Luke 11:28; John 14:21)

All things are possible with God. (Matthew 17: 20; Matthew 19:26; Mark 9: 23; Mark 10: 27; Luke 1:37; Luke 18:27)

God is our protector. (Luke 10:19-20; John 16:7-18)

Give generously and with love to others. (Luke 6:38; Luke 6:30; Matthew 5:42; Matthew 6:1-4; Matthew 25:34-40, Luke 11)

Peace is available through Jesus Christ. (Matthew 11:28-29; Matthew 1:27; John 6:33; John 14:1-4)

Jesus heals all sicknesses and diseases. (Matthew 8:16, Matthew 9:6-7; Matthew 9:35; Matthew 15:28; Mark 1: 34, Mark 6:56, Luke 13:12; Luke 6:10-11; Luke 6:19; Luke 4:40-41; Luke 5:12-13; Luke 7:10; Luke 8:2; Luke 8:48; Luke 17:14b-15)

God does not reject sinners. (Matthew 9:13; Mark 2:17; Luke 7:37-39; Luke 5:31-32)

Our spiritual enemy, Satan, is defeated through Jesus Christ. (Matthew 4:9-11; Matthew 8:28-33; Matthew 28:18; Luke 4:8; Luke 10:19)

Jesus has power over death. (Luke 7:14-15; Luke 8:53-55; John 11:25; John 11:43-44)

Finally, let us be encouraged by Jesus' last twelve words: "I am with you always, even to the end of the age."
–Matthew 28:20b (NKJV)

The Other Side of *Through*

"The LORD is my shepherd; I shall not want. He makes me to lie down in green pastures; He leads me beside the still waters. He restores my soul." –Psalm 23:1-3a (NKJV)

It's inevitable that all of us will face trouble. No matter how hard we try it cannot be avoided. When I was much younger, I believed that doing good and being in right standing with God would mean I wouldn't have to go through trouble.

I soon learned that no one is exempt from trials and tribulation. As I matured, I learned that God often uses it to develop our character as well as to build our spiritual muscles. The key to getting to the other side of through without losing our sanity or faith is staying focused on God's love for us rather than our discomfort or pain. We must never think that God loves us less because we face difficult circumstances.

In fact, God loves us so much that He wants us to be better than we were before. We are works in progress and trouble is one of the tools he uses to help us become wiser, stronger, more compassionate, etc. When we accept that God is with us through every uncomfortable moment, we will have peace. On the other side of THROUGH is always something better and bigger.

Remember, "...all things work together for good to them that love God, to them who are called according to His purpose." –Romans 8:28 (KJV)

The Power of Choice

"Call unto me and I will answer you and tell you great and unsearchable things you do not know."
–Jeremiah 33:3 (NIV)

One of the biggest lies being told these days is that we are a product of circumstances beyond our control. While it might be true that we are born with certain propensities and natural impulses, the truth is that we have the power to CHOOSE whether or not we will become slaves, chained to our socio-economical, physical and/or emotional state at the time of our birth.

In spite of the complex mélange of factors (both biological and environmental) that affect *how* we are, we have the ability to choose the final outcome of *what* and *who* we ultimately become. In other words, we have the power to do and be whatever we choose regardless of how we are born. Over the years, I have had people from varied walks of life confide their innermost thoughts with me.

Many of these people were grateful that they hadn't succumbed to all of their "feelings or desires". They had learned that their will to do what was right and helpful for themselves and others was greater than whatever forces trying to get them to surrender to their sublunary compulsions. In fact, the more they practiced their God-endowed gift to CHOOSE good over ego, the weaker their struggles became.

"I call heaven and earth as witnesses today against you, that I have set before you life and death, blessing and cursing; therefore choose life, that both you and your descendants may live; that you may love the LORD your God, that you may

The Power of Choice

obey His voice, and that you my cling to Him, for He is your life and length of your days..." — Deuteronomy 30:19-20a (NKJV)

It is tragic when people believe they are eternal victims to anything. Our world is in its most wretched state because people have propagandized the fallacy that we are predestined due to the circumstances of our birth. The fact is that we have the free will to say a loud, emphatic, "NO" to thoughts and behaviors that inevitably destroy both body and spirit.

With God's help, we can conquer any struggle and live victoriously with peace within and around us. The same amount of time and energy it takes to trespass against God and others is no greater than what is needed to do the opposite. We must not let anyone deceive us, it is easier to seek God's guidance and truth to do what is right than it is to find people to affirm our transgressions. In the end, God's way leads to a more fulfilling life. His way is the cure for depression, confusion, suicide, etc.

As we continually invite God into our hearts and let His choice be our own, the more we will experience a peace that surpasses our human understanding. We must seek Him out and He will strengthen us. Our victory is guaranteed when we walk with Him.

"God always gives His best to those who leave the choice with him."-Jim Elliot

The Power of Forgiveness

"For if you forgive people their trespasses [their reckless and willful sins, leaving them, letting them go, and giving up resentment], your heavenly Father will also forgive you."

-Matthew 6: 14 (AMP)

You have probably heard a million times that you need to forgive yourself and others. However, knowing *what* we need to do is often less difficult than understanding *how* to do it. Forgiveness is not just an ideal; it's a requirement of God. Our Heavenly Father forgives us, and as reflections of Him, we must emulate His behavior. But, how do we do it?

Ask the Heavenly Father to help you. Don't deceive yourself into thinking you can do anything by yourself. It is God's grace and mercy that permits us to do everything, no matter how small or grand the task. We need God. Our loving Heavenly Father is able and eagerly willing to help each of us do whatever is necessary to live a spiritually abundant life. Ask God to heal you of negative memories. Ask Him to restore your joy. Ask Him to reveal His understanding and perspective of your situation.

Pray for people. We must be mindful that our prayers aren't selfish. We must always pray for others, especially those who have hurt us. Those who are sick and hurting need the most successful physician in the universe—God. Intercessory prayer gets results. Just remember to pray for people as fervently and lovingly as you would want someone to pray for you.

The Power of Forgiveness

Face the truth that memories don't ever completely evaporate. Only disease and death destroy memory. To forgive doesn't mean you will forget. It means if you remember, you are healed from the pain of your past. Moreover, when God heals your heart, you are able to find treasures in your trials. He was and still is in control of your life. There is always a reason that He allows us to endure painful experiences. God never wastes our pain. There are so many rich lessons He wants to teach you through your hurt.

Make the effort to understand. Many of our actions are based on what we know and do. In order to fully forgive, we must understand. Understanding looks beyond the surface of things and helps us to dissect the "why" of situations. This takes great spiritual work and time. However, in the end, understanding why can lead to personal empowerment and fulfillment. You can't solve a problem without knowing the causes.

Finally, meditate on these powerful thoughts about forgiveness.

"Forgiving does not erase the bitter past. A healed memory is not a deleted memory. Instead, forgiving what we cannot forget creates a new way to remember. We change the memory of our past into a hope for our future." - Louis B. Smedes

"He who covers and forgives an offense seeks love, but he who repeats or harps on a matter separates even close friends." -Proverbs 17: 9 (AMP)

"There is no love without forgiveness, and there is no forgiveness without love." - Bryant H. McGill

The Power of Forgiveness

"Sincere forgiveness isn't colored with expectations that the other person apologizes or change. Don't worry whether or not they finally understand you. Love them and release them. Life feeds back truth to people in its own way and time-just like it does for you and me." - Sara Paddison

"If we [freely] admit that we have sinned and confess our sins, He is faithful and just (true to His own nature and promises) and will forgive our sins [dismiss our lawlessness] and [continuously] cleanse us from all unrighteousness [everything not in conformity to His will in purpose, thought, and action]." -1 John 1: 9 (AMP)

"The weak can never forgive. Forgiveness is the attribute of the strong." - Mahatma Gandhi

"Be gentle and forbearing with one another and, if one has a difference (a grievance or complaint) against another, readily pardoning each other; even as the Lord has [freely] forgiven you, so must you also [forgive]." -Colossians 3: 13 (AMP)

"Without forgiveness life is governed by... an endless cycle of resentment and retaliation." - Roberto Assagioli

"And whenever you stand praying, if you have anything against anyone, forgive him and let it drop (leave it, let it go), in order that your Father Who is in heaven may also forgive you your [own] failings and shortcomings and let them drop." -Mark 11:25 (AMP)

The Power of Memory

"Forgiving does not erase the bitter past. A healed memory is not a deleted memory. Instead, forgiving what we cannot forget creates a new way to remember. We change the memory of our past into a hope for our future."
— Lewis Smedes

Memories are incredible gifts from God. **Our memories are so powerful that only two things can erase them: disease and death**. In fact, no matter how hard we try to completely forget certain experiences, we cannot. Memories are either somewhere in the forefront of our consciousness or hidden behind the barrage of thoughts we entertain every day.

Good memories bring us joy; they encourage and inspire us to do more good. We find pleasure in conjuring them up repeatedly and sharing them with others. **Only when we allow it**, bad memories can potentially rob us of many blessings including peace, hope and love. While memories can be effective teaching tools, so often we choose to meditate on our bad and unpleasant aspects of our past instead of choosing to envision a positive future for ourselves. When this happens, we often suffer with shame and guilt that leads us to falsely believe that we have lost God's favor and love.

Some people can't receive or give love because of distrust, anger and/or fear. These emotions are generated by memories of negative experiences. Whenever people haven't made peace about their poor choices and the suffering that followed, and/or the sins committed against them by others, ugly thoughts of the past will haunt them and linger in their minds like ghosts that can't be seen with natural eyes, but always make their presence known through their own emotions and actions.

The Power of Memory

Even without trying, hurt people often see every new person they encounter as a potential conspirator of pain, and the toxic energy created in the past is projected into the present. Furthermore, they allow fear, suspicion and bitterness to overwhelm and damage relationships. This makes it impossible for love to flourish in their lives. Then, when relationship after relationship fails, a new batch of bad memories is added to the already mounting pile. This can lead to feelings of hopelessness and defeat.

Confronting bad memories is one of the most productive actions we can take to stop the dangerous cycle of sabotaging relationships. In other words, we have to get the courage to do spiritual battle against negative thoughts. It is our faith that supersedes our fear if we let it. The good news we are guaranteed victory with God who has NEVER been defeated. Any war against His children is already won. When we stand still (stop trying to fight everything ourselves) and let Him do the work on the inside, we will produce good fruit (actions) outwardly.

Additionally, instead of trying to avoid or suppress painful thoughts, we must ask God to show us how to manage them. Don't listen to people who exclaim, "Just get over it!" This implies that letting go of bad memories is easy when it is not. People who dismiss our memories as nothing are actually trivializing our pain.

While triumphing over trouble is very possible, for most people it is difficult. Recovery isn't something we can do spontaneously, in an instant. Real healing involves a long and arduous process of sorting out and working through a myriad of emotions. We cannot do this alone. We need God to teach us. He cannot do this if we are not good students; when we

The Power of Memory

are talking when He wants us to listen; when we don't trust Him; when we refuse to follow His direction.

We must understand that because memories are embedded in our brain's hard drive, suppression doesn't remove them; it only hides them temporarily. There is nothing we can do to stop them from resurfacing because memories cannot just evaporate into no-where land. Anything we see, hear, feel or say can randomly, without intentional provocation, trigger a pleasant or painful memory. This is how God created us. Memory like everything else He has made has a purpose. Again, it is a gift from Him.

However, God has also given us the gift of vision — to mentally create a new future for ourselves. It is important for us to move beyond the past and envision a future where we are not prisoners of our pain but free agents of love.

Memories, even the most disturbing ones, don't have to paralyze us from enjoying mentally, emotionally, and spiritually healthy lives. It might be hard to believe, but our unpleasant memories can have just as much positive power as our joyful ones. The bad ones can teach us of what not to do; and from whom to flee and avoid.

Some therapists encourage people trying to break their drug addiction to remember their lowest point. The objective of this activity is to remind the person of the pain so they will resist spiraling downward again. However, therapists also remind those suffering of the power of visualizing a future that is free of addiction and defeat.

The Power of Memory

At this moment, affirm that your life will be filled with joy and peace. Ask God to heal you and show you how to use your memories as a catalyst for positive change in your life. Declare that you will no longer be imprisoned by inner turmoil because of bad memories! Tell yourself as many times as necessary that God wants you to be free to enjoy every dimension of your life.

"[God] will wipe away every tear from their eyes, and death shall be no more, neither shall there be mourning, nor crying, nor pain anymore, for the former things have passed away."-Revelation 21:4 (ESV)

The Truth about Love

"And you shall know the truth, and the truth shall make you free." — John 8:32 (NKJV)

As with many issues, lies are the cause of so much avoidable pain and discontent. Getting the truth about anything, especially love, and transforming our thinking based on that truth, is the key to getting and keeping the love we need and desire.

A distorted view of love generally comes from the false paradigms people are taught over extended periods of time, especially during their childhood when they were most naïve, impressionable, and vulnerable to believing falsehoods.

Moreover, when people grow up in an environment littered with abuse, neglect, or abandonment as children, their circumstances often become normalized, and it is common that these people become conditioned to accept and even expect the very worst of human behavior. What happens to them externally gradually starts to chip away and destroy an already fragile or undeveloped inner identity and sense of self-worth.

This explains why many survivors of abuse grow up falsely believing that their treatment is justified in some way — they believe their mistreatment is a reflection of who they are.

When caretakers and parents don't demonstrate unconditional love and acceptance, particularly during critical periods of our emotional development, we begin to internalize the notion that we are worthless and undeserving.

During our youth, we learn to accept whatever treatment that we are given. The behavior we tolerate is indicative of thoughts, feelings, and attitudes about who we believe that we are during that particular phase of our lives. If

The Truth about Love

our sense of self-worth is healthy, we will demand the best of human behavior. If it is not, we are likely to accept abuse and disrespect.

Unfortunately, many of us carry the heavy burden of a negative and warped image of ourselves until we develop and nurture the cognitive, emotional and spiritual sophistication to realize that mistreatment is NEVER deserved or justified no matter what we do. People who maliciously hurt others do so as a result of their own ignorance, weaknesses, or pure unadulterated evil.

The truth is that while we cannot always control what happens to us, especially as children, we can CHOOSE to respond to our past and present circumstances in a way that does not eternally bind us to pain. Even though all of our experiences potentially impact our lives in either a big or small way, the truth is that they do not determine the final outcome of the level of joy, love and peace we can have.

The gift of choice enables us to decide that we will not live as victims, and that we are not limited by other people's failures, irresponsibility and immorality. God has given us the ability to choose to accept His truth: that we are His beloved children. His desire is to give us all that we need, especially love.

How God sees us is the only truth and without it we will never be able to give or receive true love. Once we align our thoughts about ourselves and others to God's thoughts, we can begin to heal our damaged hearts and minds. Because many people unknowingly become intoxicated with the illusions of counterfeit love, the "real stuff" continually evades them.

The Truth about Love

The truth is that while healthy relationships add joy, beauty, and fulfillment to our lives, it is inevitable that all human beings will experience heartache and disappointment even from the people they love the most. In spite of our good intentions and burning desire to love, we get hurt and hurt others, a countless number of times throughout our lives.

No matter how righteous, noble, loving and pure our hearts might be, all of us have flaws. Even though we can have long-lasting and fulfilling relationships, it is impossible for them to be perfect and pain-free.

However, is love the real culprit of our pain? Or do the symptoms of love's number one nemesis—selfishness, create dissension and preventable conflict in our relationships? Perhaps it is the myriad of misconceptions and distortions about love that lead us to so much trouble. Some might conclude that the senseless and selfish acts of oppression, discrimination, hatred and violence which have devastated our world throughout history reveal just how little humans know about the most powerful force in the universe—love.

Whereas lies are the root of brokenness and anguish, the truth liberates us from the emotional and spiritual bondage inhibiting us from understanding what love is, and what it is not. Only the truth about love empowers us to freely give as well as receive it unconditionally. False information though can lead to wrong thinking and destructive actions in an effort to obtain love. Thus, we unintentionally limit or restrict the flow of it in our lives and succumb unnecessarily to spiritual brokenness, depression, addiction and even death.

The Truth about Love

It is important to note that merely *knowing* the truth about love is not enough. It is also necessary to go beyond knowledge, move towards complete acceptance and finally, take constructive action. It is unlikely that love will ever manifest in our lives until the three-part process (knowledge of the truth, acceptance and action) is completed.

Most of us can't count the number of times we have heard the old adage, "knowledge is power". However, this is not true because only *applied* knowledge leads to power. In other words, if we have information (knowledge), but we fail to *use* it, we will remain impotent and powerless to positively change our lives.

Here's a case and point: If people learn how to swim but fail to employ all the lessons they learned after diving into a pool, they will likely drown. Swimmers have to accept that moving their arms and legs and breathing correctly allows them to stay above water. Additionally, they must respond to what they've accepted with constructive action — swimming.

Although I don't focus on it, I can never forget that there was a season in my life when I harbored such a limited and distorted view of love. I would not have recognized it if it had slapped me in the face. The lack of love had depleted my already compromised reservoir of self-worth and self-respect. My sense of personal identity was at ground zero which sometimes made me a human magnet for toxic people.

The lies that I believed about love made me a prisoner of the demons of my abuse-filled past. I was so emotionally and spiritually weak that it was almost impossible for me to sustain healthy relationships. Blame, un-forgiveness and

The Truth about Love

resentment paralyzed me from getting the love I wanted and needed. I eventually discovered that my long prison sentence of tormenting memories was
self-imposed. I didn't understand that "I" held the key to the shackles put on me as a child. I could emancipate myself by choosing to focus on the treasures hidden beneath my troubles.

Freedom came when I surrendered to God, the Author of Love. I discovered that He was the Master of my mind, body and soul. I no longer had to be a slave to what others thought, said and did. God had always been there, loving and holding me, even if I hadn't recognized it.
He knew what I had gone through and had planned to use all of my experiences — even the bad ones, for His glory.
He taught me how to forgive and why it is the pre-requisite to healing. He helped me to take ownership of my own mistakes and shortcomings, and not focus on other peoples' offenses.

The more I focused on God's love for me, the less comfortable I felt blaming others for my failures and problems. One of the most powerful lessons I learned was that **love doesn't come from people, it comes *through* them.** God, not people, determined my worth and my destiny. Most importantly, God taught me how to use my pain to inspire and to teach — to help people hurting as I once was. Many years ago I set a goal to create a thousand moments of joy for every tear I shed as a child.

Getting the facts about love helped me to take full responsibility for the quality of my life. The truth allowed me to finally recognize, and joyfully embrace the love that God had divinely embedded in my heart, long before my parents

The Truth about Love

had conceived me. When I discovered the truth about the power of forgiveness, the most important ingredient for enduring the arduous process of healing, I could begin to experience a love that surpassed my most beautiful dreams.

Today, love emanates from the presence of God in my heart and all around me. The love that I celebrate and enjoy is available to anyone who desires it, including you. This love is not contingent upon what other people think and say about you; it's not dependent upon what they do to you. God's love is immutable, immovable, and limitless. We are born with this amazing love indelibly tattooed on our hearts whether we know it or not.

It is with great love and hope that I continually pray that each reader of this book will discover the same awesome and preternatural creator of love that I have. Learn for yourself that Susan Taylor's words are true: "Love heals everything; nothing good is ever lost. Choosing love over ego, anger and righteous indignation takes consistent work."

"Whoever does not love does not know God, because God is love." —1 John 4:8 (NIV)

The Vine

"I am the vine; you are the branches. If you remain in me and I in you, you will bear much fruit; apart from me you can do nothing." –John 15:5 (NIV)

One school year I was blessed to receive a grant to do a special program for my students. This was something I had always wanted to do and I was so grateful for this opportunity. This award, however, came with major responsibilities and duties. I was reminded of the scripture," to whom much is given, much is required."(Luke 12:48) I received that honor to serve and although my heart was totally into the project, self-doubt about my inadequacies began to try to rise within me. I kept asking myself was I really the right person for the job. However, I used my faith and petitioned God to work through me.

I know that I am merely a vessel for His work. God assured me that if I clung to "the Vine", I could do more than I imagined or dreamt. God blessed the project. The students were successful, empowered and enriched as I had hoped they would be. This was due to God's grace.

We must remember that true success only comes when we trust and depend on God. God compensates for what we cannot do; He directs our paths and strengthens us to do His will.

I am elated to say that because I decreased, God increased the effectiveness of the program. I look forward to doing bigger and better things next year as God guides me. I recognize that I am powerless without God's help.
God is like an electrical outlet. An electronic device simply won't work without a connection. While a battery might allow use of the item, its power is limited. We must be

The Vine

spiritually hooked up with God in order to function at our maximum level. Our power is temporary when its source comes from something else.

Finally, Jesus said, "If you remain in me and my words remain in you, ask whatever you wish, and it will be done for you." (John 15:7 NIV) Believe and God will do great things through you!

Transformation

"And be not conformed to this world: but be ye transformed by the renewing of your mind, that ye may prove what is that good, and acceptable, and perfect will of God." - Romans 12:2 (KJV)

Personal transformation will not happen spontaneously or merely because of desire. It involves intentional effort, time and spiritual wisdom. Moreover, trying to change without God is like attempting to drive a car without wheels. It's not going to happen. Whenever people try to change by employing only their own human strength, their results can be temporal and unsuccessful.

However, when we surrender to God, He will direct and guide us on what, how, and when to do what is necessary to renew, restore, and reshape our lives according to His perfect will. We must remember that with God all things are possible. We can be comforted that after loss. God is willing and able to transform our minds in order to help us see what we have gained.

Continue to build the right relationship with Him and your life will be transformed in a myriad of beautiful and amazing ways.

"Moreover, I will give you a new heart and put a new spirit within you; and I will remove the heart of stone from your flesh and give you a heart of flesh." — Ezekiel 26:36 (NAS)

True Beauty

"Do not let your adorning be external—the braiding of hair and the putting on of gold jewelry, or the clothing you wear—but let your adorning be the hidden person of the heart with the imperishable beauty of a gentle and quiet spirit, which in God's sight is very precious."
–I Peter 3:3-4 (ESV)

I once had a woman in her early 30's share with me (after a volatile and dramatic breakup with one of two of her four children's father) that she wasn't worried about *getting a man*. She proclaimed that because she was "pretty and smart" she had several suitors for a relationship. Today, it's quite common for women to feel that their physical appearance guarantees them a chance to get a man.

Moreover, businesses and people who provide services or products promising to enhance one's physical appearance generate trillions of dollars each year. As I reflected on this woman's comments, I decided to share a few lessons to consider about true beauty and relationships.

While physical beauty might attract a man, it won't necessarily mean you'll get treated better. Good-looking women get lied to; cheated on; mistreated; abused; and killed every day.

It's no secret that many men want women who they deem physically attractive. However, good men desire more than just a pretty face and body. A good man wants a woman who is godly, respectful, kind, humble… I don't know too many men who would be happy with an empty-headed, selfish, immoral, and vain woman.

A man has to value a GOOD woman in order to treat her right. In other words, a woman could be endowed with

True Beauty

both physical and spiritual beauty, but if a man can't discern her worth, she won't be appreciated and/or treated well.

Finally, women shouldn't neglect taking care of their bodies, but in addition to looking good, women should invest in nurturing their inner beauty. Humility, kindness, selflessness ... don't develop spontaneously. Women must intentionally seek out ways to make sure their beauty also comes from the heart.

"People are like stained glass windows, they sparkle and shine when the sun is out, but when the darkness sets in, their true beauty is revealed only if there is light from within."
–Elisabeth Kubler-Ross

Value Your Time

"Teach us to number our days that we may gain a heart of wisdom." —Psalm 90:12 (NIV)

Nowadays, it is quite common for me to see roadside memorials. Each time I pass one, I am reminded of how fragile our human bodies are. However, I also wonder how many of those people's lives were lost *before* they received the flowers, stuffed animals, balloons, gifts, etc. Were they showered with those same gifts when they were living? Did they know how much they were loved and appreciated?

The truth is our days are short. This knowledge should encourage us to demonstrate our appreciation and love for others while we have a chance to do so. In other words, we should give people their roses while they can smell them. How much more beautiful our world would be if we told people what they meant to us when they could still hear our voices? How much joy could we create if we showed our appreciation (in big and small ways) to the people who support us? When our loved ones have passed away, they cannot hear our kind words or experience our love for them.

While it is good to commemorate and honor our beloved who have left us, let us also be mindful to celebrate people while they are alive. When we do what is right by people today, we are free of guilt and regret of lost opportunities tomorrow during the days our beloved are no longer with us.

"But do not overlook this one fact, beloved, that with the Lord one day is as a thousand years, and a thousand years as one day." —2 Peter 3:8 (ESV)

Wait!

"Have you not known? Have you not heard? The everlasting God, the Lord, The Creator of the ends of the earth, neither faints nor is weary. His understanding is unsearchable. He gives power to the weak, and to *those who have* no might He increases strength. Even the youths shall faint and be weary, and the young men shall utterly fall, but those who wait on the Lord shall renew *their* strength; they shall mount up with wings like eagles; they shall run and not be weary; they shall walk and not faint." –Isaiah 40:28-31 (NKJV)

When we call upon the Lord, He is faithful to do something. He will either calm the storm or He will calm His child. In other words, God will change our circumstances or He will change us. During most of our experiences God wants us to work on ourselves before He changes our scenery. Therefore, it is imperative that we *wait on* God as well as *wait for* Him. Waiting on Him means that we keep serving Him no matter how difficult things appear.

We continue to be faithful by being God's ambassadors through love, compassion, charity and fellowship. When we wait for Him we place our hope in God. We believe that He is our deliverer, our provider, and our source of comfort, wisdom, and love.

No matter how bad the storm is we take shelter in God's big arms and believe that in His perfect timing the storm will cease and the winds will calm. This knowledge strengthens us and restores us. It allows us to smile anyway. We will endure the storm instead of being destroyed by it.

And, we can be confident that God will bless us with whatever you need and/or desire during the right season of our lives and not a moment sooner. This is the hope that

Wait!

allows us to wait patiently with a cheerful heart. In the end, we are better than we were before because we both *waited on and for*, Our Loving God.

"The LORD is good to those who wait for him, to the soul who seeks him." — Lamentations 3:25 (NIV)

Welcome Positive Change.

"Do not be conformed to this world, but be transformed by the renewal of your mind, that by testing you may discern what is the will of God, what is good and acceptable and perfect." –Romans 12:2(ESV)

    I believe it is almost impossible to separate healing from change. Change can improve situations, but it can also make things worse. In order to experience *positive change,* you must be open to receive it. Remember, how you think will determine what you do.

    Change is generally uncomfortable because it involves the unfamiliar. In order to change, you must trust God. God is always concerned about your well-being. He will meet you where you are, but He is continually trying to help you reach higher levels of spirituality.

    When you welcome Him, you are welcoming positive change in your life. Remember, some stress is optional. You have the power to determine the quality of your life. Investigate ways you can excavate the things in your life that are harmful, unproductive, and unnecessary. Petition God for the courage to let go of the people and things that cause problems and turmoil you don't need.

    "Do not be anxious about anything, but in every situation, by prayer and petition, with thanksgiving, present your requests to God." –Philippians 4:6 (NIV)

Whose Test Is It, Anyway?

"And after you have suffered a little while, the God of all grace, who has called you to his eternal glory in Christ, will himself restore, confirm, strengthen, and establish you."
—I Peter 5:10 (ESV)

While having a conversation with one of my beloved friends whom I have known since childhood, she lamented over the problems she was facing at her job. As I listened, I couldn't help wondering if what she was going through was a part of someone's "life test". You see life is like a classroom. God loves us so much that He is always working to make us better than we were the day before. Many of our experiences both good and bad are simply tests.

God gives us tests to assess where we are spiritually. He wants us to fulfil Jesus' teachings in Luke 6: 27-38. However, sometimes we are a part of someone else's test. God is using us as vessels to give the people around a chance to be reflections of His divine love and grace. How they treat us lets Him determine exactly where they are spiritually.

During these moments, we must hold tightly to our faith; do good; and continue to demonstrate righteousness regardless of what others are going. We must keep our eyes on God; and our hearts connected to Him. Ultimately, we are victorious.

Jesus was sent to the Earth to save mankind. God was able to determine who were willing to accept or reject Him through His son. The "stone which the builders rejected" was a part of humanity's test.

In the end, in spite of Jesus' rejection, he was victorious and became the chief cornerstone. (Psalm 118:22) How did he

Whose Test Is It, Anyway?

do it? Jesus depended upon His Heavenly Father. Jesus once said, "I can of Myself do nothing. As I hear, I judge; and My judgment is righteous, because I do not seek My own will but the will of the Father who sent Me."--John 5:30 (NKJV)

What a powerful example for us. We must emulate our Savoir whether we're facing our own test or someone else's. We must not let our spiritual enemy distract us from focusing on God and do the will of our Heavenly Father who justifies us. Be encouraged! All will end well for you! My dear friend shared the praise report that God has opened new doors for her!

"Abide in Me, and I in you. As the branch cannot bear fruit of itself, unless it abides in the vine, neither can you, unless you abide in Me. I am the vine, you are the branches. He who abides in Me, and I in him, bears much fruit; for without me you can do nothing. If anyone does not abide in Me, he is cast out as a branch and is withered; and they gather them and throw them into the fire, and they are burned. If you abide in Me, and My words abide in you, you will ask what you desire, and it shall be done for you. By this My father is glorified, that you bear much fruit; so you will be My disciples. As the Father loved Me, I also have loved you; abide in My love." –John 15:4-9 (NKJV)

Working as God's Agent

"A good man out of the good treasure of his heart brings forth that which is good; and an evil man out of the evil treasure of his heart brings forth that which is evil: for out of the abundance of the heart his mouth speaks." - Luke 6:45 (KJV)

Each of us has specific and general assignments from God. Through prayer, we can fulfill God's purpose for our lives and do great good for His kingdom. With His strength, guidance, and comfort, we can rise above our carnality and adversity to accomplish extraordinary feats.

Whenever we are trying to do the right thing, we need to call on the Lord. He is faithful to hear us. God transforms our mind and heart so we are empowered to do the most difficult of spiritual tasks. We don't serendipitously do good; we do so by trusting and leaning on the Lord.

Our Heavenly Father's power increases in our lives, as we decrease our carnal desires. In the end, we are successful — we are victorious because we depended upon God and we surrendered to His will and His way.

You don't have to be perfect to work as God's agent. You just need a willing heart to serve Him. *His* perfection will cover you; His grace will keep you from complete destruction. Throughout history, God has used men and women who made mistakes, and those who even forsook their walk with God.

Beloved, decide today that establishing and maintaining a relationship with God is the most important thing you will ever do. He loves you unconditionally and accepts you just as you are. As your relationship becomes stronger, you gain the strength you need to do His will. Each day of your life pray to God for guidance, protection,

Working as God's Agent

provision, wisdom, and everything you need. Only through Him can you complete your divine purpose. I hope the following prayer by Saint Francis of Assisi (c.1181 – 1226) helps you draw closer to God.

> "Lord, make me an instrument of Your peace;
> Where there is hatred, let me sow love;
> Where there is injury, pardon;
> Where there is error, truth;
> Where there is doubt, faith;
> Where there is despair, hope;
> Where there is darkness, light;
> And where there is sadness, joy.
> O Divine Master, Grant that I may not so much seek
> To be consoled as to console;
> To be understood as to understand;
> To be loved as to love.
> For it is in giving that we receive;
> It is in pardoning that we are pardoned;
> And it is in dying that we are born to eternal life."

X-ray Your Heart

"Search me, O God, and know my heart: try me, and know my thoughts: and see if there be any wicked way in me, and lead me in the way everlasting." –Psalm 139: 23-24 (KJV)

There have been times when I looked beyond the outer layers of my heart and found a malignant, spiritual tumor that needed to be removed. So often, the by-products of selfishness, dishonesty, jealousy, deceit, etc. build into a hard mass of sickness that we unconsciously keep deeply behind the fear of facing the truth.

The truth is that human beings are selfish by nature, and must have supernatural help to operate above this natural inclination. Trying to be unselfish without God is like trying to lose weight without reducing your caloric intake. Some might do it, but the results are generally short-term. X-raying your heart means closely inspecting the core of your spirit.

When you find a tumor, a by-product of selfishness, you must have it removed. Let God be the surgeon.

Introspection is an integral component of long-term spiritual growth and healing. Only with the highest levels of spiritual maturity can a person admit his/her mistakes. It takes an even greater level of spiritual level to positively work to improve oneself. Using a spiritual x-ray allows you to see what's not easily visible and beneath the surface of your heart.

"Let us draw near to God with a sincere heart and with the full assurance that faith brings, having our hearts sprinkled to cleanse us from a guilty conscience and having our bodies washed with pure water." — Hebrews 10:22 (NIV)

Yield to God

"Therefore submit to God. Resist the devil and he will flee from you." — James 4:7 (NKJV)

Throughout this book I have reiterated that healing and spiritual growth are directly connected to God. *Who is this God, you might be wondering?* The term, God, is used so loosely today, by so many different religious groups that it is not surprising that people, especially young ones, are confused about Him.

Religious leaders with various spiritual doctrines, all proclaim that their way is the right way and the only way to God. Collectively, several groups of people have spent millions of dollars and billions of minutes trying to prove that they are right and all the others are wrong. To make matters worse, when religious leaders interpret their texts, their followers often get a combination of personal interpretation and literal meaning.

It saddens me greatly that children are the greatest casualties of these religious wars. They cannot figure out who to trust. Their parents expose them to one particular teaching, but the people next door, teach something else. God, amazingly, is often left out of the teaching! God gets lost in people's personal ambitions. So for clarification when I suggest yielding to God, please note that I am referring to the Creator of the entire universe.

Yield to God

God, a preternatural source of power, is the indisputable Creator of the planets that *man* (humankind) has yet to see; the sun that man will never touch and the millions of life forms that man will never completely identify. Anything man makes has the potential to break down. Our cars, houses and computers are all made by man. Man, trying to be God, has spent untold fortunes trying to clone animals and humans, namely his selfish idea of perfection. But man will never be able to duplicate the moon.

And, no matter how hard man tries to forget, God always reminds humans of their finite power; people will die and there is nothing they can do about it. God, on the other hand, is the Eternal One. He will never die. He has been around for quadrillion light years before man, and He will be here long after man destroys himself.

Yield to this God. Trust in Him. Get to know Him for yourself; do not merely take my word for it. He will guide you to the people, places, and resources to ameliorate your spiritual life. He has been waiting to envelop you with His awesome love and power. Do not reject Him.

"Do your best to present yourself to God as one approved, a worker who has no need to be ashamed, rightly handling the word of truth." — 2 Timothy 2:15 (ESV)

You Will Live

"I called upon the LORD in distress: the LORD answered me, and set me in a large place. The LORD is on my side; I will not fear: what can man do unto me? The LORD taketh my part with them that help me: therefore shall I see my desire upon them that hate me. It is better to trust in the LORD than to put confidence in man. It is better to trust in the LORD than to put confidence in princes…I shall not die, but live, and declare the works of the LORD."

-Psalm 118:5-10, 17 (KJV)

At some point in most people's lives, we will lose a relationship with a beloved person. This can happen as a result of death as well as from a divorce or excommunication. While this experience is usually very painful, it is possible to live without a person with whom we once shared a close bond. Our destiny is not determined by people who will leave us. Our fate does not rest in the hands of those who will intentionally hurt us.

We must take the lessons and memories gained from past relationships and discover how to use them to make us stronger, wiser, and better. We can live — in fact, well, if someone decides to walk away from our lives. Our health, joy, peace, etc. is created by God. Of course, God works through people to manifest His will, but He never wants us to be totally dependent upon them for our security and wellbeing.

The scribes of the Holy Bible encourage us to trust God, not men. God is faithful to bring the right people in our lives in due time. We don't have to hurt ourselves and others because of the loss of a relationship. When our heart aches, we must ask God to help us heal.

You Will Live

We must seek His guidance for how to look forward to the bright future He has in store for us. We must be confident that He will transform our pain into a purpose. We will live to tell the testimony of our triumph over loss when we trust in God.

"He who dwells in the secret place of the Most High shall abide under the shadow of the Almighty. I will say to the LORD, "He is my refuge and my fortress; My God, in Him I will trust." — Psalm 91:1-2 (NKJV)

Zoom in on Self-love

"Letting go of negative people doesn't mean you hate them. It just means you love yourself." — Unknown

You have probably heard the expression: "If you do not love yourself, no one else will." This could be one of the biggest spiritual fallacies known to mankind. It *is* possible for people to be loved by others even when they do not love themselves. Nevertheless, what is true is **that if you do not know what love is, you will not recognize it when it is being expressed.** In fact, you might even reject pure agape love because it is so unfamiliar to you.

Self-love is important because it removes your dependency on other people for your personal happiness. When you love yourself, you are no longer pre-occupied with trying to *find* it. Here are some facts to remember for life: people cannot *make* you happy. **They are incapable of supplying all of your needs because they are imperfect; they make mistakes; they are complex. When the quality of your life is *totally* dependent upon other people, what is going to happen when they inevitably do something wrong? When you place unreasonable expectations on people, you create misery for yourself and others.**

Your spiritual needs must be deep inside yourself. That way when someone is having a bad day, you will not; when someone is depressed, you won't need to take a painkiller! Zoom in on self-love. Accept that you are a reflection of God. God is love.

"This is how God showed his love among us: He sent his one and only Son into the world that we might live through him. This is love: not that we loved God, but that he loved us and sent his Son as an atoning sacrifice for our

Zoom in on Self-love

sins. Dear friends, since God so loved us, we also ought to love one another." — I John 4:9-11 (NIV)

God wants to heal you from the effects of broken relationships. Seek Him out for wisdom, peace and most importantly, His everlasting love. God is able to transform your life in amazing ways that stretch far beyond what you could envision or think. Will you let Him?

"By this we know love, because He laid down His life for us. And we also ought to lay down our lives for the brethren. But whosoever has this world's good, and sees his brother in need, and shuts up his heart from him, how does the love of God abide in him?" (1 John 3:16-17 NKJV)

Acknowledgements

Heavenly Father,
What could I do without you? Absolutely nothing! So, I thank You for being my faithful Rod and Staff.

Felicia,
For the past 26 years, I've been blessed to call you "daughter". Thank you for being my most enthusiastic cheerleader and encouraging me to keep writing.

Mary,
On behalf of my students, I cried for help and you answered. I am grateful that God allowed you to be a blessing to them!

Family,
I have been blessed by each of you in very special ways. I am a better human being because of our special connection.

Suzanne,
Thank you for this beautiful cover!

Salvation Army,
You gave me my first Bible. Most importantly, you taught me (and hundreds of disadvantaged youth) about the story of Jesus Christ as an act of God's unconditional and unwavering love for mankind. For this, I am infinitely appreciative.

About the Author

C. Chérie Hardy was born and raised in Florida. She is an award-winning educator and inspirational speaker. Her life-changing and encouraging messages about overcoming obstacles and strategies for achieving personal success have motivated thousands of young people.

Hardy has also worked as a voice personality for several theatrical productions including, "The Present Day Ruth".

Morning Chai with God: Inspirational Messages that Strengthen Your Faith is C. Chérie Hardy's eighth book.

The author is the proud parent of one daughter who is also an aspiring writer. She and her family currently reside in the Atlanta metropolitan area. Feel free to send your questions and comments to the author at: **ccheriehardy@gmail.com**

Other Books by C. Chérie Hardy

Daily Pearls: Inspiration and Wisdom for Each Day of the Year

Encouragement for the Grieving Heart: 365 Uplifting Quotes and Scriptures for Coping with Loss.

Love Doesn't Hurt: Life Lessons for Women

Teach. Learn. Inspire: A 180-Day Inspirational Journal for Teachers

The Orange Zebra (First Children's Book)

The *Orange Zebra and The Kind Giraffe*

The Power of Gratitude: 365 Quotes and Scriptures for Healing Your Mind, Body, and Heart

Three Nights in December (First Novel)

Wise and Wonderful: Life Lessons for Single Mothers

Available now at
www.avantgardebooks.net

[1] Information about the pearl was retrieved from http://science.howstuffworks.com/zoology/marine-life/question630.htm on January 5, 2013.

www.ingramcontent.com/pod-product-compliance
Lightning Source LLC
Chambersburg PA
CBHW060157050426
42446CB00013B/2872